ARCHITECTS
of
LIGHT

ARCHITECTS
of
LIGHT

as channeled by
Sharon Shane

Liquid Light Center

Liquid Light Center
www.sharonshane.com

First Edition published October 2004

ISBN # 0-9676968-2-8

Interior Design/Typography: Sharon Shane
Cover Design: Juergen Neckenich
Illustrations: Sharon Shane
Author Photo: Mathu Andersen

Printed in the United States of America

In Service

to the

Beloved

One

TABLE OF CONTENTS

I N T R O D U C T I O N

◇◇

During the channeling of "Architects of Light," I endeavored to keep as clear a channel as possible to bring forth this message with as much succinct clarity as I have known the Ascended Masters, the Master Creator God beings, and host of Spiritual Guides to impart through my telepathic rapport. It would not be possible for me to channel this information other than through the vehicle of my own Higher Consciousness. Among the many Masters that I am in communion with are St. Germain, Lord Sananda, Yogananda, Quan Yin, Djwah Kuhl, and my own personal guide Ascended Master John, as well as many councils of wisdom keepers. The Master Creator God being, Thoth, is ever coaxing me onward to comprehend the numerical formulas of dimensional frequencies with always a dash of unique humor and Divine Love that spans eons.

In the midst of this cooperative effort with the Ascended Masters and the Spiritual Guides, I was engaged in applying the mastery technique of one-pointed consciousness described in this book by focusing all of my intent to bring forth the information. In the trilogy of books that I have authored to date on behalf of the Ascended Host, my own path of mastery and dedication as a World Server has become clearer to me with each endeavor.

Engaged in the work aligned with my path of Higher Purpose I am always learning from the Masters each step of the way. Upon bringing forth this information, I am in awe and also delighted as the many missing pieces of the greater puzzle are revealed to me. My task as scribe to the Masters offers me the many gifts of the teachings. As they say throughout this work, the rewards are in our alignment with Higher Purpose.

At a few times within this current body of work, the reader

will notice that the Ascended Host uses phrases like, "We have already taught you, etc." It is their way of not repeating the same information in this written work that was already put forth in the previous two books, "In the Garden of the Goddess" and "The Rhythm of the Cosmic Pulse." Although "Architects of Light" can stand on its own with much for the reader to absorb, it is also to be noted that it appears that the Ascended Host is building upon each work with more depth of multidimensional meaning to what has been taught previously.

Because many of the sentences are so succinct, they are literally packed with multi-dimensional layers of meaning. Therefore, some of the paragraphs may not seem to flow and they may appear to come to an abrupt halt at the end of a sentence only to begin another sentence that brings you to another halt. I have been telepathically informed that this material was presented in this fashion for a reason. The Ascended Host advises that you relish each sentence to glean the most of the wisdom that is offered in each line. Every sentence is meant to be slowly pondered and savored for its rich content rather than hurriedly scanned like a speed-reading course. Therefore, pay attention to any sensation of feeling halted when you reach the period at the end of some sentences. Those are the moments you should stop and reread that sentence to gain a fuller depth of meaning from the words. In these channeled works, there are many multidimensional layers of meaning to glean with each reading. As I have come to love and understand from the Ascended Host, their play on words is intended to be both fun and meaningful. We are reminded to have fun with the word play but to not overlook the layers of powerful meaning to be found in the subtle nuances. Although the entire volume is replete with knowledge and wisdom, it is this author's intuitive sense that the first and last chapters were dictated so the reader could take a sentence or paragraph at a time in no linear order. They appear to be as bookends made out of sheer wisdom enfolding the more linear presentation of the chapters in between, which offer more teachings of the creation principles.

It is always this author's intent that the material put forth represents the highest truth possible imparted through this means. If the material falls short, it is only due to my own personal limitations on the path of mastery and in no way reflects any shortcomings on the part of the efforts of the Ascended Host.

Sharon Shane

P R O L O G U E

And there came to pass a child was born within the poverty and dust of the cities of metal and cement, and this child was born with the knowing of things to come and the things that once were. The cries from its voice were muffled in the cacophony of the urban squalor. Each day the child grew, its voice became stronger. Then another child arrived born within the beauty of the jungle gardens, and this child was born with the knowing of things to come and the things that once were. Its voice was lifted on the song of nature, and each creature knew this song and sang along in harmony. Each day, as the child grew, its voice became stronger. It became so strong that the child within the city heard this same song singing through a bird perched on a building ledge high overhead. The city child knew the song and began to sing along. Now the people walked by on the busy city streets and the child went unnoticed. No one heard the song, but still the child sang in unison with the child in the jungle. Together their voices became stronger. Then there came to pass a child born on the savanna, and this child was born with the knowing of things to come and the things that once were. This child was born singing the song, and the creatures of the plains sang loud and mighty along with the child. The child in the jungle and the child in the city heard this new child's voice. This lifted their voices stronger, and they all three sang the song in unison. As the child in the city grew and watched the city walls falling, the voice of the song deepened but still continued singing. A passerby stopped short in their tracks and listened to the city child singing the song. Then the passerby heard the bird on the ledge high above the city streets singing the same song. The passerby heard the child in the jungle and all the creatures blending in singing along with the child on the savanna and all the creatures there also. The passerby was moved to tears and began to remember the song and sang along. Soon a crowd gathered around the passerby and the grown child on the city street to listen to the beauty of this song. One by one each person in the crowd began to remember the song, and they all joined together in unison to sing. A mighty chorus was now being born and their voices lifted so brilliant that the people in the next town stopped in the midst of their daily chores to wonder at the strains of beauty filling the air. They too began to sing this song until one by one every person in the world joined in the chorus. This was the day of fulfillment. The day of the ego had long passed. The truth of the present was always with them, and the future of vision had been fulfilled, and so they all set about the work of the new creation.

ONE

THE NEW CREATION

*When the clarion call is sent forth, there are those
that resound with the joy of World Service.*

Hear us now say this is the time of the planning. Hear us now say this is the time of breaking new ground. Hear us now say this is the time of laying the foundation of times to come.

What is the new creation other than a world that has never before been actualized on earth from the foundations of Divine Love? What is ascension but the lifting up of the earth on the wings of the dove? What is Divine Plan but the fulfillment of the perfected design of human divinity? Who are the architects of Light but the unified efforts of the Ascended Host with the workers in the Light on earth?

We speak now to bid you hearken to these words for within each word are the seeds of potential. Within each seed are the multidimensional layers of evolution designed through the blueprints of Divine Plan. We speak now to awaken you to your power and to guide you to align your consciousness with the Ascended Host in cooperation to bring forth the next phase of Divine Plan.

We have taught you that Divine Plan is creation and evolution occurring concurrently. The pulsing rhythm of Divine Plan is experienced at a different pace in your world than is experienced from the perspective of the Ascended Host. Therefore, we hold in our hands the Divine Plan blueprints that span eons and offer to you a page at a time so to speak. Blueprints are but an outline that you will build upon. We offer these guidelines for you to begin with the foundations of the new creation. The foundations are to be built on the ground of being.

Faith is the foundation of belief. Beliefs shift and crumble, but the foundation of faith must remain steadfast. Therefore, when beliefs begin to shift and crumble, do not dismay that you will lose your footing as long as your feet rest firmly upon faith. Faith is not fantasy. Faith is not fancifulness. Faith is the basis of trusting that which is beyond your present sight. We do not speak of blind faith. Blind faith is reserved for the spiritually naïve. True faith is unshakable. We speak of the faith that knows without a shred of doubt that it is already accomplished. We speak of trusting that the table is prepared before the guests arrive. Responsibility of the workers in Light is to align unwavering faith in Divine Plan in unison with the Ascended Host. Faith in the highest vision is not seeing the way things are but seeing beyond into the highest potential of creation. This is a simplified formula of synthesis to follow in claiming your role as an architect of Light. Faith is a necessary component in the foundation.

Ignorance gives birth to ignorance. Ignorance is the father of sloth and laziness. We speak in reference to spiritual laziness. These traits have no place in the new creation. Those who entertain petty notions hold their soul's evolution in suspension. Only they can free themselves from their own shackles. As the way shower, a worker in the Light must become a beacon shining the truth upon earth so others can find their way out of the darkness of ignorance.

Do not be distracted by the clamor of turmoil around

you. Let not the false prophets of fear and separation cast a shadow across your path. Follow not the lead of those who proclaim that to divide is to conquer. Worship not at the feet of those that preach fear. Neither place no other on a pedestal above you. Sweep trepidation from your doorstep. Follow only where the heart leads towards the unification that is Divine Love. Walk in the radiance of a clear and loving heart, and the Light will shine upon thine countenance. Fear is the doubt that casts shadows upon your smiles.

Many are the days that have been squandered upon fascination of the ego's enticement. These days cannot be recaptured, but do not despair for a day in your time is but a speck of dust in the universal scheme. Let it be known that each day that is squandered is merely a postponement of reaping your greatest rewards. One must seek in order to be found. Each day you delay the seeking of your Higher Self is another day you will remain lost. Welcome yourself home in the heart of Divine Love.

Seek not that which entertains the ego's fancy. Do not chase after illusions. Seek nothing that is less than the eternity and infinity of Divine Love. Make the effort towards embodying Divine Love your utmost goal in each and every word followed by action. Many are the ones that are forsaken in the quagmire of their own illusions. Bold are the ones that shine the Light of their own brilliance.

Seek only that which is aligned with truth and all remnants of false matter will fall to the wayside. Truth is found in the fulfillment of Higher Purpose. When you are aligned with Higher Purpose, you will know the truth for you will be the truth. This is not a work for the faint of heart or the worshippers of fear. Those who are called will answer. Those who cannot hear the call are the faint of heart and the worshippers of fear.

3

Their ears are deaf and their hearts are closed. They are the detractors and naysayers. Pay no heed to such distractions. They are those who have placed their faith upon the sands of shifting times rather than crossing the threshold into the eternal Light. Those that walk in the shadows of their own dark ways cannot see the Light that is their own becoming.

Those who respond to the call are the workers in the Light in service to humanity on behalf of the One Source. Do not misunderstand the term "World Server" with your interpretations of slavery or servant. Stand tall in your grace and dignity. Hold your heads as high as the principles that you adhere to. Among the group of the World Servers are the visionaries, the prophets, the sages, the Light bearers and Light weavers, the keepers of the flame, the dream weavers, the truthsayers, the empaths, the healers and the compassionate ones. Tarry not your mindset to be concerned with these as titles for the World Servers. They are but terms to acknowledge the worker in the Light by these traits they embody. Workers in the Light well know their tasks and chosen roles through the application of the gifts of these traits in service to humanity. There are no ranks other than the ranks of the truly devoted. Devotion to Divine Plan is the first prerequisite for those who shall bring forth the fruition of unification. Devotion rests on the rock solid foundation of faith. Together they reinforce the cement of the foundation. We do not refer to the same understanding of your foundations in the buildings of cement you erect on your plane. When we reference the phrase "cement the foundation," it is to help you understand that the bonds of Love and devotion are mightier than the sword of hatred and division. There is naught that can put asunder the bond of Divine Love for all is truly One.

We address the World Servers by saying we encourage

you to ask the Ascended Host for help and strength in your endeavors, but we also encourage you to ask how you can better serve the Ascended Host. In accord with the maxim, "Ask and ye shall receive," ask how you can better serve the Source in the carrying forth of Divine Plan and the door to your path of Higher Purpose will open. The asking is the begetting. The chosen are those who choose.

Step up boldly to the threshold of the next level of your awakening and do not hesitate to step over. Hesitation is a distraction of fear. Should you hesitate in taking the next step, we are ever patiently waiting with a helping hand to guide you into the next realm. What is a realm but the boundaries of your own limitations? You are the one that decides the boundaries, for you are the one that creates the limitations. Your world is created from boundaries. Shift your boundaries by shifting your perception. When you feel locked within your stagnant ways, walk around yourself and view yourself from another angle. What do you perceive about yourself that you had not seen before? If you still feel like a blind man groping in the dark, call out and we will hear you. Do not anticipate how we will respond but be open to receiving.

The door you seek is always open, yet you believe it is locked and bolted. Ask yourself sincerely, "Would Divine Love lock you out from its warm rays?" The very essence of Divine Love is the warmth of the Golden Solar ray upon the Silver White beam of reflection. We ask you again to look upon the waters of the Self and see if the reflection is clear. When you see the Golden White Light, you will understand clarity. There is no fog but that of your own confusion. Confusion arises from the lack of trust in your own Higher Knowing. Wander not through the confusion of the maze you create but step now fully into your power. To continue listening to the ego's voice is a choice made by the ego. Discern which voice you listen to. Move the ego to the backseat and let your Higher Self take the wheel of the vehicle. We refer to the vehicle as your four-body system. When the ego drives the body, the body responds to limitation. When the ego drives the emotional body, emotions erupt without warning. When the ego drives the mental body, thoughts ramble on about how to limit your experience of your indescribable magnitude. Discern the voice and shift gears. Let the Higher Self coordinate your focus of consciousness through all realms.

To be of service to the One it is always and ever the gift to bring the energies of Divine Love into the world in every day things. Kind words spoken to strangers can open up gateways to the stars. A simple glance of warmth can convey the meaning of eternity. Bread offered to one can satiate the hungering masses. Fortitude and strength can support the weary. A peaceful countenance will calm all worries.

Each foot placed upon the path must be placed with gratitude. Each step taken must be taken in trust. There are no pitfalls other than the trenches of your own inner conflict. Inner conflict creates rifts in consciousness and thereby creates rifts in human affairs. There are no roadblocks other than those you place before you. The path is smooth, and the way is open. Any barrier you encounter is a reflection of your own limiting belief. Shatter the barrier by expanding or shifting the belief. Expand your consciousness beyond belief and into the realm of pure faith and trust in knowing it is already accomplished. These are the traits of mastery, and you are all Masters in your own right. Stand in your own center and be not swayed. Precisely the moment you understand and apply these principles of truth is the precise moment you vivify the Master within.

That which brings together in unification is that which is the essence of Divine Love. That which tears asunder in separation is that which is the petty meandering of the ego. The time of the ego is past. The time of truth is present. The time of visions is future. The time of Love is always. To Love in all ways is the Love that is always.

Hear us now say that the time of choosing between the path of the ego and the path of World Service is nigh. We have said it before, and we will say it until you embrace the truth in the words that proclaim, *"You cannot serve two Masters."* Those who serve the ego's purpose do not serve Divine Plan. Those who serve the ego delay their own participation in the work of Divine Plan, but even they cannot delay a plan that is so Divine in its design as to include for the delays of those who choose to tarry at the altar of the ego.

We speak of this again and again to impress upon you the understanding that there is no evolution within the limitations of the ego. The human ego overly inflated in its self-importance yet deflated of spiritual power by its inherent limitations is out of step with the evolutionary rhythm of Divine Plan. Quieting the voice of the ego makes way for the voice of the Higher Self. Aligning with the pulsing rhythm of evolution through creation will bring you in accord with your greatest truth in each moment.

Possibilities are infinite, but there is one path free from debris. When you weary of moving boulders, you will step upon this path. Then the way becomes Light. Pave the road with righteousness to ease the burdens of those that follow in your wake. Whosoever walks in the center of truth makes the way Light.

A heart on fire is a heart fulfilled with purpose. Many are those that walk in the shadows of a closed heart. Few are those that emanate the shine of the emerald heart glow. Let the heart fires of Divine Love illuminate your world. Can you not see that your own radiant Heart is the Light that opens the passage through darkness?

The new creation has never been. You are those that will seed the embryo of the new creation. You are both the seeds and the embryo. The new creation will be birthed from the focussed discipline of one-pointed consciousness. One-pointed consciousness takes the discipline of mastery, and birthing the new creation takes the mastery of Group Soul endeavor. You are those that will midwife your own births. When seeds of the stars are placed in the soil, what else will blossom but the brilliant Light of a sun?

There are those who follow the paths of religions. There are those that follow the path of ancient ritual, while there are those that put their faith in old wives tales and superstition. Understand that there are always lesser truths within the Greater Truth, and we advise that you pay no heed to superstition or ritual steeped in the baser thought formations of the energy of fear. Follow only the rituals as guidelines that bring you to the center of your Self. We ask that you be tolerant to all who are in their own pace of evolution. Tolerance is the key to honoring the multitude of diversity with the many within the One. The elementary teachings of religions and belief systems have had their rightful place in humanity's history to teach the basic principles of the truth, but look beyond to see how they can also be entrapments and limitations for you and others to continue to adhere to.

It is nigh time for the workers in the Light to take the next great leap into the truth and knowledge that is your spiritual and physical heritage. Fusion of the first through fourth dimensions into the fifth, sixth and seventh to create the new heaven on earth is the beckoning call we herald to you. Yes, we are well aware that you hear the proclamations that the fifth dimensional portals have opened, and we commend you on your excitement of these initial stirrings of your stellar awakenings. Yet we are here to alert you to the reality of even more dimensions of consciousness and energy for you to expand into.

Again we urge you not to confine yourself by limitations. Awaken your cells, rally your forces of instinct into the halls of command, and be ever masterful in your duties. Be all of these things and more. Be all of who you are and then stretch even beyond that. Yet we must also guide you to remain on your spiritual toes and be ever the discerning seeker upon your path to learn how to attune to that which is the highest truth that you can embody at any point of your focus. Discernment is the guidance of the intuition that is impeccable.

Beauty is only born out of the wisdom that treads delicately on the soil of seeds freshly planted. Proclivities toward engaging the forces of disruption hinder all progress. Seeds planted will sprout in their own season. The cycles are ever turning, and the leaps of evolution are upon you. Tilling the soil of human consciousness prematurely before the seeds take root creates confusion, and the garden will be rife with the weeds of contention. A garden is only as fruitful as the quality of the seeds planted and the gardener's tender and nurturing attention. Plant seeds of value and the crop will reap its fruit. Healthy seeds reap an abundant harvest. Cultivation takes patience and attention. Patience is long-standing while fortitude is its anchor. Treat each one with nurturing care, and the garden will blossom in brighter hues of human wellbeing. Fruits of the labor not tasted fall too far from the tree. Dig your roots in deeper and let the soil nurture your thoughts. Then the well streams of wisdom will be like the sap flowing in your veins extended to each leaf, and the fruit that you bear will be an oasis of refreshment to the weary traveling Soul.

Clarity is to truth what falsehood is to a muddy pond. Look upon the waters of the Self to see if the reflection is clear. Swim in the ocean of your own depths without fear of drowning in the abyss. Thereupon you will uncover the treasures of your Soul. It is not enough to uncover the treasures for what good is their beauty locked in the treasure chest lying on the ocean floor? Swim to the surface and let glimmer in the sunlight all the beauty that is hidden in the darkness of the unconscious realm.

Energy directed through Divine Will is power. True power does not falter. True power does not waver. True power does not vacillate. Harnessing true power and directing idealized vision toward manifestation is one-pointed focus of consciousness. The true power of one-pointed consciousness aligned with the vision of high ideal is the tool needed to lay the foundations for the cities of Light. The power of faith, devotion and trust combined can move mountains. Mortars and fire rockets can also move mountains, so how much greater it is to use this power of faith, devotion and trust to alleviate all suffering. The time for the cycles of destruction is nearing its end, and the time to rebuild is upon you.

Within the text are the words of truth, but within the spoken word are the deeds. All words spoken are deeds of action and impact. Every syllable holds the powers of creation in its resonance. Spoken words ripple forth on the breath of life. Life impacts life. All deeds reap a harvest, but not all that is harvested are nutrients to the Soul. The meaning of "choose your words carefully" is the alignment of your intent with the highest purpose prior to speaking. The words, "I'm sorry," can be empty from years of habitual response or may be filled with the real healing sorrow of remorse. Saying you forgive someone without the release of the blocked energy of hurts inflicted will not bring about unification. Empty words keep the doors to the heart_ locked and bolted. Truthful intent is the key that turns the lock. When the door of the heart is open, the floodgates of Love are unleashed. Reap only that which feeds the Soul and nourishes the Spirit, and the garden will be bountiful. Water the garden with words of kindness, and Love will bloom. Words of detraction feed the weeds of anger and hatred that choke the roots of Love. Positive endeavors birth positive outcomes. Negative intent wreaks havoc upon the land. An act of genuine kindness unravels the threads of the worn out fabric of hate. Where there is an empty field in consciousness, plant the crops of awareness. Be the tillers of the soil of consciousness. Reap the rewards of a bountiful garden.

The new creation is manifested through mastery. Mastery over the senses precludes the mastery over the intellect. The reasoning faculty of the intellect makes way for intuition. Intuition aligns the consciousness with serendipity. Serendipity aligns with synchronicity. Rhythmic pulsation sets the tone of creation. A symphony is born.

Ascension is the raising of the frequency rate of thought vibration. The new creation is manifested through telepathic rapport. There are always two choices. There is the choice to align with the energy of fear or there is the choice to align with the energy of Divine Love. There is the choice to align the thought patterns of the ego with other egos, or there is the choice to open to the channel of the Higher Consciousness and align the thought patterns with the Ascended Host. Telepathic rapport with the

Ascended Host and with the other workers in the Light will bring about the manifestation of the new creation. Thought patterns of vibration must be raised to the level of resonance that resound truth, beauty, grace, integrity and peace through harmony. Let this be the song of your Soul. Let this be the echoing refrain that carries forth the sound of creation.

Through the law of frequency, the number of workers in the Light will increase in accord with the frequency to which you are attuned. What do we mean by this? The level of your frequency vibration will attract those of like vibration. As you raise your resonance higher, it will inspire and encourage others to reach beyond their present resonance. They in turn will uplift others and this brings humanity exponentially to a higher resonance in steps and stages. When you find yourself surrounded by the detractors and the naysayers, do you join in their ranks to rally the plight of the separatist beliefs or do you stand on the solid rock of the unifying principle? How easily do your branches snap and break in the winds of discontent? With how much frequency do you apply your knowledge and wisdom? How frequently do you practice your skills of mastery? In your world of definition and redefining yourself, these are samplings of measurement for shifting your resonance to a higher frequency vibration. In this way, you can attune your awareness to when you are aligned with Source in the present moment rather than wavering on the threshold of the beckoning ego. When you shift your resonance to the higher thought vibration, you are a beacon to those around you. You only need to watch over your own actions rather than concern yourself with the actions of others. Lift yourself above the old foundation so that others may be lifted in your presence to stand on the new ground alongside you. Walk among the people and spread your

Light on the wings of the dove.

Many roads are traveled but few find their way home. Fumbling in the darkness of their own limiting thoughts many cannot see the Light that shines like a beacon within the center of their own consciousness. You must become the Light of awakened consciousness at the center, and then the rays of truth will Light the land.

When the eyesight is turned within in meditation and inner contemplation, do not tremble in fear to behold the *All-Seeing Eye* of the Creator looking straight at you. To look within is to see your Creator. The eye of the Creator is ever upon you. It is you who have turned your back on your Creator. Some of you have seen this singular eye and were startled. Do not fear looking Love in the eye, for it is in the singular eye that Love is beheld. The eye that is split in two are the eyes that see double. Seeing double is to take up sides. When you wish to co-create aligned with Divine Plan, simply turn within and look the Creator in the eye and in the "I." The "I" that is you will see the "I" that is the "I AM THAT WHICH I AM," and you will know in your Heart of Hearts that you and the I (eye) are One.

Fingerprints are laid on a surface, but, until you dust for the fingerprints, they cannot always be detected. The fingerprint of the Creator has touched the face of humanity, but humanity must recognize the fingerprint as its own.

When you close your eyes and look within, see the threshold. It is not hard to discern, as it is the shining brilliance of your own countenance. Step into this Light and bask in the glow of your own brilliance. Step into the arms of Divine Love and know you are home.

Step into your rightful place of honor alongside the Masters. At the threshold of the throne you will find your Golden scepter of power. Do not hesitate to lift it high for it will Light the way for all who still fumble in the darkness of their own ignorance and fear. Time is of the essence we say, for time is the essence of your becoming. On your level, time must be perceived as patience for Divine Plan takes the patience of eternity.

Awaken all ye Masters and know this to be truth. Truth must be claimed if it is to be proclaimed. Embody the truth and all words uttered forth will echo its refrain. The foundation of the new creation is built on the ground of being. Be the truth, walk the truth, live the truth and the truth will be known. Step into mastery. Know.

This is the clarion call. Who among you shall resound to this call with joy?

TWO

MASTER PLANS

*Bricks to be laid are Golden
but not of the metal that is mined.
Silver is the cord that will unbraid
the strands woven by time.*

There is no enigma greater than to solve the mystery of evolution. The mystery cannot be solved unless you become involved. There is no place for passive observers in the new creation. Full conscious participation is mandatory.

The template of times to come is the template of times undone. The foundation cannot be overlaid upon the old way for the rocks of ages past are crumbling to dust. The old way must be dissolved to make way for the new. To dissolve the old way is to solve the enigma of evolution. Walls that must crumble are the invisible structures of belief systems steeped in fear. A belief in the enemy is a belief steeped in fear. A belief in poverty is a belief steeped in fear. Greed is an abuse of power, and its underlying motivation is a fear of powerlessness. To worship the ego is to worship fear and separation for the ego perceives through the eyes that see double. Unless thine eye be single you shall continue to perceive separation. There is no simpler way to state this highest of truths. The only enemy is fear. The only poverty is living the ego's life that fears the reunifying with

Divine Love through the Higher Self. Fear destroys all efforts towards unity. This is why we encourage each and every one of you to confront your own dark fears first and foremost. This is why we state succinctly that there is no place for the ego in the work of the World Servers for the ego's battleground is fear. To conquer the inner enemy of fear is to ensure peace within. Inner peace creates resonant waves of harmony. Inner peace creates a harmonious external environment. Walk not in the footsteps of fear but rather take bold new steps to create a world of Love. Therefore, raising your resonant vibration above fear is primary to the new creation.

A prophet is not born out of the ordinary path but chooses to enter into the path of prophecy. They are the heralders of the blueprints of high ideals. Templates and blueprints are designed in the realm of idealistic vision by the Elohim and the Master Creators. Divine Plan is transmitted telepathically via the Masters and the Ascended Host and imparted to the Higher Consciousness of the visionary, the prophet, the sage, and the teachers of wisdom. It is the task of the visionary, prophet, sage and wisdom teacher to plant the seeds of the vision in the soil of mass consciousness. It is not enough to simply plant the seeds. Seeds take root when the workers of Light nurture the seeds. Weeds of negative patterns that choke off the roots of growth must be removed. Any and all thoughts and purpose not aligned with Divine Plan and Divine Love must be vanquished.

Orchestration of Divine Plan cannot be fully detailed in books or otherwise. Evolution of species, planets, solar systems, universes and the greater Cosmos span much more than Light years. It is not possible to contain eternity in a mason jar. In comparison to the Cosmos, the perception through the ego's limiting view can be likened to trying to fill a mason jar with an entire ocean, and yet even this metaphor is lacking for the im-measurable simply cannot be measured.

All possibilities contain all possible outcomes. Who is to say which way you will choose until you choose it? Who is to say what you will create in your world until you make your choice? This is the power of choice. This is the reality of multi-dimensional consciousness. We use the metaphor of traveling down a road and coming to a fork in the road. One way leads right, and the other way leads left. When you choose which way to go, you perceive that your choice sets you upon one path over the other. Your perceptions are based upon the limitations of your beliefs. We are here to tell you that even though you believe you choose one way over another, you are still travel-ing down both paths. Would you even begin to believe us that when you step fully conscious into the sixth dimensional fre-quency of creation that you can consciously experience both the right path and the left path simultaneously. It is not inherent in the energies of Divine Love at Source to limit your experi-ences of choice. Further beyond the sixth dimension you can begin to experience not just the limitations of two choices but the freedom to experience multiple realities simultaneously. All paths exist because the freedom to choose exists. Even to stand still at the fork in the road is a choice. Perhaps you choose to pause and ponder. Then you may choose to continue walking. Observe that as soon as the choice is made, the way is made clear. There are layers of meaning in this statement. Ponder these things. Thoughts are cloudy and kicking up dust. Ques-tions of which choice to make spin in circles in your mind until you get frantic with dizziness. Take notice that as soon as you make a choice, any choice, the way becomes clear because you have become clear enough to make a choice. The dust settles enough for you to see clearly through to make a choice. It is that simple. Sometimes you just leap off the metaphorical cliff and pray that your parachute will open. It always does, because all choice made on any level of consciousness is simply transition and shifts of focus. Consciousness is eternal and infinite and is always in transition for nothing remains static. This also means that creation is eternal and infinite and is also always in transition for nothing remains static. Furthermore, this also means that the All That Is of eternity and infinity is also always in transition for nothing remains static. How can it not be that what is true on one level of consciousness does not permeate all of consciousness? Where would the separation begin and end in the One that is all things made manifest and all things non-manifest and all things yet to be made manifest? Choice is a powerful tool in the new creation. The fear to make any choice at all is to choose fear. Do not berate yourself for the choices made. If you are unhappy with the choice, you can always choose again. Within the freedom of one single choice is the power of the creation of a million suns. What lies before you is a palette of colorful choice. Hasten to release the belief that you are limited to only the primary colors of creation.

We do not address the issue of choice without further addressing the issues of intent and impact. With every choice made come degrees of responsibility. Some choices made have greater and far-reaching impact on the self and others. Other choices made have lesser impact. You might think that being a decision maker in the world and choosing to enter into war brings a great deal of impact. We would tell you this is an accurate assessment. What you may fail to see is that what you may call the ordinary man or those who are not in the position of being a decision maker for a nation of people have an equal level of responsibility in their choices. We refer to the difference between everyday little choices of choosing what to have for dinner and being faced with life's greater challenges that have a higher level of impact. A leader of a country can choose what dinner to order from a menu, and he/she can also choose to take up arms against another nation. Likewise, the ordinary man/woman can choose what dinner to order from a menu, and he/she can also choose to take up arms against his/her own family in the way of verbal or physical abuse. It is the challenge of the emotional belief system we refer to when making choices and not the position in society that one holds. Great men/women are not made from the office they hold but from the little everyday choices they make that are aligned with spiritual integrity of the highest degree. Character, integrity and human dignity are the traits to embody on the spiritual path. The ability to respond to the choices made with integrity in all matters is a marker on the path of spiritual mastery. Responsibility should not feel heavy. Rather spiritual responsibility makes you Lighter. It is the enlightened being who bears the most responsibility for he/she is the embodiment of the Light that is intelligent self-awareness. Each choice and action taken by the enlightened being must be aligned with the utmost integrity. Enlightenment and responsibility walk hand in hand. With each initiation mastered, you inherit more power. Power is not bequeathed until the consciousness has evolved to the level of Light that is equal to the level of power.

The Master blueprints of Divine Plan are the purest, visionary ideals of spiritual essence seeking to be made manifest throughout every layer of multidimensional consciousness. It is not to say that all is predetermined in the outcome of implementing these efforts. What is predetermined is that the highest ideals will always and in all ways seek to find expression in form. This is the basis of the Master plans. Divine Love seeks to find its highest vibration of expression through the multidimensional tiers of creation. The design of the form of the new creation is intended to be in closer alignment with the purity of spiritual ideals than in previous endeavors, but only if the World Servers put all efforts towards alignment with the ideals herein outlined. We remind you again that not all of the details of Divine Plan can be limited to the written text for that in itself places limitation upon the efforts of the Ascended Host and the workers in the Light on your plane. Divine Love is flexible. Therefore, Divine Plan is flexible for there is no separation between the two. Divine Love flows like all rivers that open into the ocean of infinity. Even to address you as separated on your plane is a paradox worthy of attention for it is you that sees through the eyes that are double, while we endeavor to enlighten you to the reality of unification through the eye that is singular. Thus, we must continue to speak your language to bridge the gap in your perceptions until you awaken to embodying these truths and claim them as your own. The structure of a sentence is linear. Multidimensional reality is non-linear. Applying the structure of a linear sentence to a description of the abstracts of multidimensional reality is a limitation. However, each letter, syllable and word in each linear sentence contains the vibration of multidimensional layers of meaning. Until you awaken and master the truth of your multidimensional nature, we must still work within the confines of your limited dimensional arena of conscious participation. With each step, we guide you closer to the core of experiencing your own truth.

Divine Tasks

Because there are many tasks within the multidimensional tiers of consciousness to carry out the manifestation of Divine Plan, we offer an outline in accord with the basic formula of the creation principle. The Ascended Host herein sketches the template outline, but you will color in the details by your own design. This is the beauty of our co-creation work together. Here we give you more paradox to wrap your minds around for we delight in anticipation to see which colors you will choose to radiate in all your glory, yet we recognize you by these very colors.

It is the task of the keepers of the flame to ignite the passion to carry forth the dream and to keep the fires that fuel the energy of creation burning in your dimensions. This work is primarily of the element of fire for passion is fueled by a fiery intent. Golden Light of solar fire is the potently powerful raw energy of creation. We use the metaphor of the Golden bricks of solar fire as the building blocks of creation. Fire is the electric charge. Solar fire must ignite in the Heart of Hearts to connect to the human heart chakra through the fiery passion, which will then ignite the charge of the synapses in the human brain with the new imprint of higher ideal. Those concerned with this task must meditate upon the Heart of Hearts and align the human heart with Higher Purpose. The Golden Light of the solar fire thus emblazons the truth of the higher ideal upon the brow through symbol and fire letters. This in turn ignites the Heart of Hearts fusing the human heart chakra with the Heart of Hearts of the Higher Self, which then energizes the emerald heart within the four-body system. Fire codes of the Language of Light etched upon the ether are impressed from the singular "Eye of God" upon the spiritual human being's eye that is singular. Does this not bring a new meaning to you of the saying "seeing eye to eye"? In this transference are the highest vibrations of the solar fire. When the fire of passion and devotion to the Ascended Host is ignited within the Heart of Hearts and aligned with the human heart, solutions appear. Solutions appear in the eye that is singular. We draw your attention to the root word of solution being that of *sol* and the correlation with the root word of the solar sun. Solutions emanate from the fire codes at Source to varying degrees of multidimensional awareness within Divine Plan. Higher solutions are brought forth to your plane through your solar sun to see the Light of day.

A most difficult challenge for the truth-sayer is to monitor their thoughts ever so closely and choose their words ever so carefully in order to speak the highest truth into your plane. This work is primarily of the element of air, for it is on the breath that the spoken word is brought into your plane. From the threshold of the Elohim at the Holy of Holies, the most intense energy vibrations are sent forth on the Divine Breath of creation as sound vibration. The Word of creation ripples forth into streams of Silver waves. The Silver waves of the Divine Feminine Breath ripple upon the Divine Masculine Golden solar fire causing the friction of radiation. Air is the element of the static charge. Just as there are syllables and breathing pauses in your language, the static charge is what keeps the breath of creation aligned with the rhythm of cosmic pulsation. Breathing exercises to align the rhythm of the human breath with the Divine breath of the One Source is recommended when too much static disruption to the nervous system is encountered. Control of the breath to attune to the peaceful emotions will smooth out the static interruption. Understand these things that any disturbance of your thought fields will create a counter-friction. Radiation is not a negative term as in your world's present lack of understanding of the nature of the higher science of this energy. This static disturbance of the counter-friction to the higher radiating energies causes the breakdown in the transference of the reception of the new energies in your field of manifestation. The outages and disruptions in the flowing forth of your conscious intent are only blocked by the lack of understanding of these principles. Your intent is witnessed by all the goodness in your own hearts. Understand this simple formula. Do you not see the correlation of the radiation of the Source emanating the Divine principles of creation to be the same as the radiant Heart that is your inherent nature? We offer this guidance for you to align your consciousness with these Higher truths. It is a delicate balance to maintain the proper rhythm of the breath and its subsequent effects on the nervous system of the human body. Communication of "The Word" through the Divine Breath stirs the fire codes to flare and "en-lighten." The Silver braid of Divine Breath weaves the words of truth to unravel the disguise of all illusion. Solar flares ignited in your sun emitting radiation reflect this cosmic process in your solar system. When the breath of life is aligned with Divine Source, wisdom is spoken. We bring your attention to the root word of wisdom, which is "wise." As the call of Divine Source beckons across the fields of creation spanning eons with the question of *"Why?"* what else will be its echoing response other than through its reflection in the eyes that become (why-eyes) wise through awakening to self-awareness and the application of knowledge? We taught previously of the "om" as returning home to Divine Source. Creator reflects upon the creation, and the going home is the "wise – om" that is wisdom.

The healers, empaths and compassionate ones also have

a challenge of delicate balance, as they must initially use their bodily vehicles to transmute the emotions of suffering into the pure heart source of Divine Love to uplift the world in the healing process. This work is primarily of the element of water, as the emotions are purified through the cleansing process of water. Water is the element that is the conductor of the charge. When the emotions are clear and pure, the conduct is pacified. Peace is then conducted through the water channels of Gaia consciousness and the human body. Be aware that the reference to the human body is both to the personal human vehicle and the greater body of humanity, as well as the bodies of the earth, moon, planets and stars. There is no separation between them other than that which you perceive with your own limited perceptions. Meditate upon this to see the water surrounding and within your bodily cells and the oceans of the earth to be the purified waters of all life. When the waters of life are purified and pacified, there is no impediment to the outpouring flow of Divine Love.

Likewise, it is the task of the dream weavers and Light weavers to connect the web of Light by networking the global family of Light. This work is primarily of the element of the earth, for it is throughout the global network that the visions of Light must be woven. Earth is the foundation of spiritual commitment and the element of grounding the charge. When the workers in the Light walk upon the ground of commitment in carrying forth the tasks of the Great Work, the sphere of conscious influence expands. This is how the consciousness of earth expands and ascends to a higher vibration together with the spiritual human being. Grounding the solar fire through the Divine breath upon the waters that are clear and flowing brings the clarity of truth that is the higher vision to the earth plane. As the clarity is infused into the earth element in phases, the earth is transfigured into crystalline substance. From out of the crystalline substance of the new earth the crystal cities of Light shall shine forth. Understand that although the frequencies of vibration are increasing as you raise your resonance, this process of transfiguration of human and earth will occur over an undetermined span of evolution for both Gaia consciousness and humanity. All is dependent on many factors the prime of which is the workers in the Light stepping into mastery.

Unification through these elemental tasks within Divine Plan is a masterful step of yet another aspect of the foundation ground for the new creation. Those upon the path of spiritual mastery must at a certain point attain the command of all the combined elemental forces herein described. Employing these tasks into the knowledge or "the knowing" opens up the living library within the garden of all possibility that you are becoming.

The Light bearers are focussed in their endeavors to activate the Light in the new matrix grid that envelops the earth sphere. It is their task to ground the energy of the higher resonating dimensions in key points around the globe from the earth core to the meridian system of the stars. Their work takes place primarily in the etheric realms. Merging the fourth dimensional elements with the newly activated matrix grid is the integration of the fourth and the fifth dimensions. Multidimensional abstracts of sacred geometries are the map of how this alignment takes place.

Success has already been accomplished in opening the seals of the vortices that were temporarily closed to the upper echelons of the fifth dimensional frequencies and beyond. The electromagnetic grid system of Gaia consciousness has been shifted into place for the new creation. Activation along the earth's meridian points are being conducted by the workers in the Light ongoing. Mass humanity has yet to catch up. Reactions to the increasing intensity in vibration have created an excess of agitation and eruptions of emotional disharmony. This only occurs when lower density thought vibrations attached to the emotions of fear clash with the more highly refined vibrations of Divine Love being infused into the planetary grid by the Ascended Host, in combination with the raising of the resonance through the workers in the Light. Through the Law of Resonance the Ascended Host holds the resonant frequency at the new grid level, while the workers in the Light diligently raise their resonant frequencies to align. Through the Law of Resonance as the workers in the Light do not waver to lower their resonance, it will be mandatory for the greater body of humanity to raise their frequency. This is why we impress upon you the utmost importance for each of you to hold to the highest vibration you can attain for the evolution of greater humanity depends upon it. Otherwise, the recycling of history's patterns will continue to repeat and the quickening of evolution will be waylaid. As more and more of humanity becomes attuned in alignment with the newly formed matrix, this work to balance the transition continues under the vigilant and loving guidance of the grid Masters.

Of all the tasks of the workers in the Light it is of great import to understand the work to evolve matter. Throughout the evolution of the human form, there has been great need to bring the matter and Soul in harmony through the infusion of the Light to evolve matter into Divine Wisdom through the Heart of Hearts. What we refer to is the work to transmute matter into the Light of intelligent self-awareness through Divine Wisdom. Cellular memory holds all phases of the kingdoms of creation on the fourth dimensional plane within the biological substance. Within the human cells is the memory of the animal nature, the plant nature and the mineral nature. What distinguishes the human kingdom level of evolution from the animal, plant and mineral kingdoms is the ability to evolve into the spiritual human being and harness pure power to consciously create. The only distortion to the human being consciously creating heaven on earth, also referred to as the ascension into the higher resonating dimensions, is due to the limitations of the ego. We are aware that this appears a simplistic explanation in the increasing complexities of your world drama. However, be aware that the increasing complexities of your world drama are a mirror of the intense necessity to conquer the ego's fears and projections of fearful images onto the fields of manifestation that is your fourth dimensional plane of creation. Transmutation of the animal, plant and mineral kingdoms are all accomplished within the spiritual human being level of conscious awakening. We are here to tell you that it is imperative to tame the lower nature of the human animal within. This level of work is done on the emotional and mental body planes. Destruction, killing, lust, greed, envy, sloth and violence of any kind cannot exist in the new creation. Punishment of such deeds is not in the due course, but transmutation of the lower nature into its refined essence through the energy of human dignity is of utmost importance in this phase of Divine Plan.

A great part of this task called Lightwork is to consciously infuse the visionary higher ideals into the cellular memory. This is conscious work to align with the Higher Consciousness to imprint the next levels of Divine Plan into the human DNA as a new program of evolution. Purification of the four-body system to align with the twelve-body system of the Higher Consciousness is a refinement process. Elevating the vibration of consciousness to the refined vibrations of pure spiritual essence is transmutation. Work done on the cellular level is through the use of meditation techniques to align the cellular structure with that of the Light body. What other is the Light body but the body of the Higher Consciousness that is the Light at Source? In steps and stages through the refinement process, matter is elevated on its return journey to the Light at Source. There are degrees of Light Body activation in this process to become the Adam Kadmon. The quickest method to achieve the acceleration of this process is to surrender the ego's grip on fear and allow for Divine Love to work its miracles. The ego defines itself by boundaries of three-dimensional physical objects and a self-image of limitation, while the Higher Self is defined by the qualities of spiritual essence. Old limitations of boundaries imposed by the ego are replaced with the intangible boundaries of spiritual ethics and integrity. Can you now see how the ego resists giving up its own tiny definition for fear of being swallowed up in a boundless sea of pure consciousness? Are you able to embrace the paradox that your individuation process does not get swallowed up in an ocean of oneness? We would suggest you ask yourself, if that was the case, then why individuate within Divine Source at all? In steps and stages, the four-body system aligns with the twelve-body system of the Higher Consciousness as the twelve-chakra system.* Be ever mindful that the twelve is not the end point, but just another resting place for consciousness to integrate all energetic systems into more awareness of the One.

---

* For more information on the twelve-chakra system see *The Rhythm of the Cosmic Pulse, pp.106-111.*

Merging Dimensions

Within the creation principle are many tiers of sacred geometrical form. Comprehension of the higher sciences is like any other study on your plane with the additional multidimensional aspects that you have now readied yourself to understand and employ. At each new multidimensional threshold of initiation, there is a portal of consciousness to open. We will give you an introduction into the nature of the dimensional portals. A portal is an opening. What is a multidimensional portal other than an opening to the next level of your conscious awareness? What is a dimension other than a frequency of energy vibration? With each dimensional level of awareness that you are able to attain, hold and masterfully function within, there are increased intensities of energies available at each level. Take great notice that we tell you that you must be able to hold your consciousness and masterfully function within each level. Energy is pure power, and consciousness is pure awareness. Consciousness controls the energy at each dimensional level so as to use its power to direct and extend into the creation fields. This needs to be repeated for your conscious mind to grasp, for there are those of you that are able to consciously visit these multidimensional levels without having learned the ability to expand your consciousness permanently into these realms to utilize and direct these energies available to you. Therefore, do not be confused between "visiting" other dimensions and "mastering" the energy of other dimensions.

There are two basic approaches to accessing the higher dimensional levels of frequency vibration. The first is to consciously harness and work directly with the energies, and the other is to open up through meditation and allow the energies to permeate your consciousness. The first method is the most potent and takes the skill of mastery. The second method also has its merits.

We spoke in previous teachings of the seven dimensions of the creation principle within the octave of infinity. In brief summary, all of the abundance needed in the fourth dimensional experience is inherent within the original archetypal garden of manifestation of the earth plane. However, with the distortion of proportionate levels of fear reigning within the ego's domain, this creates a domino effect of fear permeating all kingdoms. You see it is not the insect's fault for stinging or biting or the snake's either. When humanity awakens to telepathic rapport throughout all the kingdoms, then there is no need for a snake to bite or an insect to sting or any animal to react viciously. When the human being conquers fear and becomes telepathically aware of the insect or the snake in its own kingdom of habitat, this completely avoids the need for the insect to react in fear of being harmed. The lower resonant nature of these kingdoms are transmuted to the expression of their higher essence within the evolutionary level of the spiritual human being. When the spiritual human being is awakened to the reflection of the spiritual essence of the Higher Self level through all four kingdoms of the fourth dimensional plane, the spiritual human being is elevated into the fifth dimension and beyond. At this level of awakening to the fifth dimension and beyond comes greater enjoyment of the freedoms and abundance of energy at each level. Until the spiritual human being awakens to these levels of consciousness through the masterful conscious intent of utilizing these frequencies, however, there will still be the issues of limitations imposed upon consciousness at the fourth dimensional level. One must expand beyond these limitations by including all of the fourth dimensional experiences within the fifth dimensional frequencies and so forth. The fourth dimensional experiences include the four kingdoms of mineral, plant, animal and human. The fifth dimension includes these four, as well as the initial awakenings to the kingdom of the spiritual human being in the realm of unlimited imagination. The fifth dimension is the realm of an endless infinity of imagination that imagines itself. All creation is imaged into form from out of imagination. Without the image conceived prior to creation, there would be no creation of form at any level of the matter worlds. From out of this pool of unlimited imagination the conscious creator conjures up images of new-sprung archetypal templates for the new creation. These fifth dimensional energies are then balanced with consciousness holding the focus within the paradoxical sixth dimension of the energies of complete stillness and a stirring chaotic energy simultaneously. At the seventh dimensional level, the consciousness includes the initial stages of the one-pointed focus of Higher Conscious mastery over the creation process.*

Now we will address the initiation of the twelfth dimensional frequencies. Twice times the sixth dimensional frequency of the merkaba brings you to the twelve. We introduce these concepts to point your awareness toward understanding that within each octave of creation are its higher frequencies. The twelfth dimensional frequencies are the higher aspect of the sixth dimensional frequencies. At the twelfth dimensional level, the Higher Consciousness works in direct communion with the Elohim to bring forth the idealistic vision into manifestation. What bodes true in all expansion of consciousness bodes

---

* For more explanation of the fifth through eighth dimensions, see *The Rhythm of the Cosmic Pulse*, pp.130-137

true to this formula of the creation principle as well, which is to say that with each initiation into higher frequencies comes more complexity and a greater deal of responsibility within the creation principle. Some of you want to run before you learn to walk, and we are here to assure you that you will all attain the initiations to the level of your ability to integrate the intensity of the frequency vibrations at your own pace. Patience is ever your companion on the path, and you would all do well to invite its company along the way.

We suggest that you first turn your one-pointed focus to master the sixth dimensional level of the personal merkaba. In its most basic function, attaining this level is to hold the duality of paradox. A three-sided pyramid represents the trinity aspect of the creation principle. Three is the lowest number needed for creation on any level of consciousness. Begin with the two three-sided pyramids joined at the base and bring your focus to the six faces or facets of this figure. Each facet is a field of Light reflection and refraction. Light of consciousness within the geometrical abstract both reflects back upon itself and also refracts in an extension of consciousness. The upward point of one three-sided triangle and the downward point of a second three-sided pyramid is the sixth dimensional challenge of concentrated focus (see Fig. 1). Next bring your conscious attention to merge the two pyramids in a centering point that is referred to as the merkaba or Star of David (see Fig. 2). In steps and stages the awareness must then be focussed to include the two pyramids times the three facets on each.

Fig. 1   Fig. 2

When a sufficient amount of mastery is attained to hold the focus at that level, then the consciousness can be expanded to include the twelfth dimensional level, which merges the spiritual human being with the earth core. This includes the personal sphere of conscious influence, as well as the global sphere and aligns consciousness of the spiritual human being to that of Gaia consciousness. These are the beginning steps of what has often been referred to as merging heaven and earth.

Now there is an iron octahedron (two four-sided pyramids top to bottom with eight facets) at the earth's core. The top four facets govern the northern hemisphere, and the bottom four facets govern the southern hemisphere. United they create the geomagnetic force at earth's core as the magnetic poles representative of the four elements and the four kingdoms, which have long been referred to as the four corners of the world.

Meditate upon this unification in this way. The awakened spiritual human being aligns the energy of their activated merkaba in unification with the iron octahedron at the core of the earth. This conscious action of the spiritual human being activates the octahedron at the center of the earth to align with the merkaba of Gaia consciousness bringing it into the sixth and twelfth dimensional frequencies. Conscious activity of the spiritual human being working with Gaia consciousness aligns the field of the sixth dimensional spiritual human merkaba with the fourth dimensional hub at the earth core. As both the spiritual human being and the Gaia consciousness are activated in unison, this sets forth an increasing accelerated solar/electromagnetic field of creation aligned with the fifth and sixth dimensions and escalates the resonant frequency of the fourth dimensional field of creation. Continuing work on the unification of these energies between the awakening spiritual human being and the awakening Gaia consciousness solidifies the new form of the new creation. Energetically speaking this creates a new foundation in the localized field of manifestation.

Fig. 3   Iron octahedron at Earth's Core
creates geomagnetic forces of revolution
prior to merkaba activation technique

Fig. 4   Gaia's activated merkaba at Earth's Core
after merkaba activation technique
unifying humanity with Gaia

It is not the purpose of this current volume of work to fully address the next leap in consciousness of the twenty-fourth dimensional frequencies to align more powerfully to the star essence.

However, we will offer an introduction to the twenty-four. Twice times the twelve brings you to the twenty-four. As we previously stated, it is not possible to contain infinity in any volume, but for all practical purposes to put into effect conscious co-creation of these principles it is quite handy to know the basic formulas.

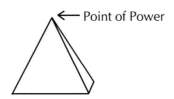

Fig. 5   3-sided pyramid + Base = 4 facets

The 3-sided pyramid in dimensional reality has four facets when counting the bottom base. Overlapping two geometrical three-sided pyramids including the base facet gives you the sixth dimensional merkaba, which in multidimensional reality also merges the twenty-fourth dimension because it creates twenty-four facets to the figure. It should appear obvious that all higher number includes the lesser number. Each facet on the geometrical plane represents a dimension that refracts and reflects Light. The basic formula for this would be:

2 (pyramids) x 4 (facets of the 3-sided pyramid) = 8

When the two 3-sided pyramids are merged into the merkaba, this gives you eight protruding points or intersections. The point of any intersection is the point of power. The more points of power focussed upon, the more powerful the outcome. What we mean by this is that the more points of power the consciousness is able to hold simultaneously and direct creation into the dimensional fields, the more powerful the creation. We will challenge you to stretch your consciousness and wonder in amazement how many points of concentrated focus are necessary to hold the universe in manifestation over the millennia of evolutionary Divine Plan?

As you look closely at the merkaba figure below, see that each protruding edge of the four faceted pyramid has only three sides visibly showing. Multiply each protruding facet as:

3 x 4 (facets to a pyramid) = 12 and then 2 (pyramids) x 12 = 24

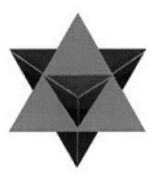

Fig. 6

Take note of the eight protruding "points" or connecting intersections of the planes and twenty-four facets or surface planes in the above figure. We remind you that each facet reflects and refracts a portion of the Light that is within. The Light emanates from within the "center-point," which is always the place of balance. Each outward extending "point" or intersection represents a single-pointed focus. This symbol of the sixth, twelfth and twenty-fourth dimensions reflects and refracts the Light into twenty-four dimensions. In actuality it is a synthesis of consciousness at the twenty-fourth dimensional level of awareness. From your perspective, it is a great stretch for you to comprehend the sixth dimensional understanding of this, for you view it from the limited third and fourth dimensional and linear perspective of a diagram on a page. As your awareness approaches just utilizing six of the facets of the sixth dimensional frequencies, perhaps you can begin to comprehend how the multidimensional frequencies of creation are layered within each other. This is a simplified example to present, as your dimensions within a book are far too limiting to reveal these scientific realities. We highly recommend that you take your conscious awareness to the next level of working meditatively with these understandings by being at the center of the merkaba energies and directing them from your center point of balance. Holding the concentrated focus at the center-point of balance on a singular ideal, as in tranquility or peace, and then directing them exponentially to the points of intersection is where the focus should be addressed. From that point of focus, the Light energy is then diffused through refraction and reflection into the fields of manifestation.

Keeping in mind there are eight "points" protruding from the merkaba and eight facets of the iron octahedron at earth's core, now envision the merkaba of the sixth dimensional spiritual human being overlain upon the earth sphere. To be more specific, envision that the earth sphere is at the center of the spiritual human being merkaba. Next envision the eight points of the merkaba directing Light to reflect off of the eight facets of the iron octahedron at earth's core. Then if you are able to stretch your conscious awareness even further, envision the sphere of the earth surrounded by the twenty-fourth dimensional figure in expression of twenty-four facets. The eight points of the sixth dimensional merkaba are aligning with the meridians of the newly shifted earth grid matrix and the facets of the twenty-fourth dimensional geometry reflect the new "faces" thus creating the next multidimensional grid for the new creation. Herein lies the explanation of the mysterious mathematical formulas we offer when we state this is the three into one, etc. With each facet added, it melds the other facets into a new dimension and a new geometrical shape, which reflects the dimensional vibration. Therefore, the term two into one or three into one or four into one merges each level to create an entirely new "one." Each creation is a new entity. Each new creation spawns more knowledge. As we state repeatedly, number is infinite and all number resonates to the depth of meaning inherent in its nature. Knowledge is infinite. As we also state repeatedly, paradox runs rampant through all dimensions. Furthermore, both sides of any paradox are simply lesser truths within a greater truth, ad infinitum. If these guidelines to the creation principles boggle your conscious mind, they are meant to, in order for you to awaken to the fact that your conscious mind is limited within the constructs of fourth dimensional thinking.

The qualities of Light are refracted and reflected through the myriad multidimensional spheres of the creation fields. Within the qualities of the Light will be found the truth to the pure essence of consciousness. Qualities are both a state of being and the energetic active dynamic of the creation principles. The essence of Light is the purity and wisdom of Divine Love. It is intelligent awareness. It is brilliance. It is reflected and refracted throughout creation in infinite number. The only distortion to the brilliance is within the fallen continuum of ego distortion, whereas the Light of creation is trapped within the density of the lower thought and emotional vibration fields of the fourth dimension.

Sacred Seals

Approaching this understanding of the sacred geometries in steps of the basics alleviates the overwhelming nature of infinite number. Meditative work on the sacred seals and symbols that follow (see Figures 7- 13) hastens consciousness to advance in its progress along the path. Be mindful that these depictions of mandalas are only limited versions of the multidimensional level of energies involved in the geometrical design. Understanding of the more advanced levels of these geometric patterns of creation comes with the ongoing expansion and depth of conscious awakening. In contemplation of the seals, allow them to act as a door to experiencing the multi-dimensional frequencies and be mindful to focus on integrating one level at a time before moving ahead to the next. Shift your inner perceptions to observe and understand the multi-dimensional nature of each seal. The seals are keys to the portals of conscious inter-dimensional travel. We offer a generalized and simplified outline of the dimensional seals here in this text, as the only proper way to enter into a greater understanding is to step into the dimensional frequencies and experience them fully conscious. The basics of this numerical sequencing of these seals from six to twelve all have higher numerical frequencies hidden within each seal. Allow the seals to act as portals to experiencing expanded consciousness.

The Seal of Solomon is the meditation on the sixth dimensional frequency of the merkaba. Much has already been said about this seal. We recapitulate as stated in previous works that this is the portal to the sixth dimension of learning to balance paradox into the "both/and" beyond the limitations of the "either/or." Always the center is the point of all balance. Meditation on this seal also prepares the way for conscious opening to the twelfth dimensional level of awareness.

Meditation on the Seventh Seal aids consciousness in directing one-pointed focus to combine the seven-chakra system within the physical body. This exercise is the unification of the seven into one. At the center of this dimensional seal is the pillar of Light that is singular with the seven Light pillars of knowledge extended into the fields of creation. There are a multitude of singular pillars of Light with seven subsequent pillars surrounding them for within each octave of creation you will find degrees of the Light that is the knowledge of intelligent self-awareness emanating from these pillars.

The Eighth Seal centers upon the eye that is singular. This meditation aids in awakening inner vision into the landscape of the Soul and the initial glimpses into the truth that is infinity and eternity. It is the portal to the higher vibration of the fourth dimension that you commonly refer to as "time." Concentration upon this seal will aid in dissolving the illusions of linear time into the reality of eternity.

Meditation on the Ninth Seal aids to open the portal to the Higher Self. Accomplishing this level of focus is to master the personal sphere of influence through the direct command of the Higher Self upon the combined four elements with direct intent. It opens the antahkarana Light connection of telepathic rapport and the command over one-pointed focus and activation of the life energies through the ongoing evolutionary program.

The Tenth Seal is that of the portal to unify the awakened

spiritual being with that of the global sphere of consciousness. The five-pointed star is the symbol of the human being. Spiritual seekers should make note of the overlapping of the five-pointed star in this Tenth Seal, whereas the fifth dimension is that of the awakening individual spiritual human being, the tenth is its higher frequency uniting the individual with all of humanity.

When meditating upon the Eleventh Seal, the spiritual human being is aligning consciousness with mastery on global awareness in preparation for World Service. Holding the one-pointed focus in the eleven points of this seal prepares the aspirant to leap into the twelfth level of focus.

The Council of Twelve represents the Elohim. However, this is not to say that the twelfth dimensional frequency of vibration is that of the Elohim, for they sit at the threshold of the Holy of Holies as a vibration that is what could be considered the nearest to infinity. Meditation on the Twelfth Seal is to align the consciousness with your Higher Consciousness at the twelfth-chakra level and the twelve-body system. From that alignment then the frequencies can be adjusted to progress towards communing directly with the realm of the Elohim. Only through absolute humbleness of any and all ego can the individual consciousness near this level of vibration to sit in awe before the throne. From the realm of the Elohim at the threshold of the Holy of Holies direct vision is imparted.

Once again we issue forth notice that each level of the dimensions outlined open up to more dimensions exponentially into infinity. It is always in your best interest to concentrate on one focus and to allow periods of integration. Holding the consciousness directed in six or seven points simultaneously is enough of a challenge than to allow the ego's frantic worry to baffle over how many more facets of dimensions this creates.

Fig. 7   SEAL OF SOLOMON
OF THE SIXTH DIMENSION

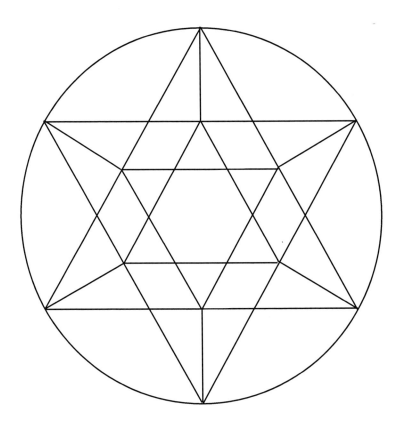

Fig. 8   SEAL OF THE SEVENTH DIMENSION

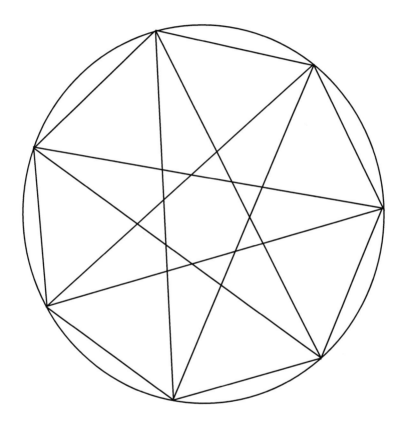

Fig. 9   SEAL OF THE EIGHTH DIMENSION

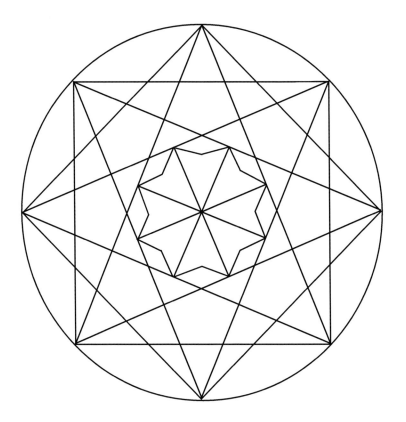

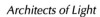

Fig. 10   SEAL OF THE NINTH DIMENSION

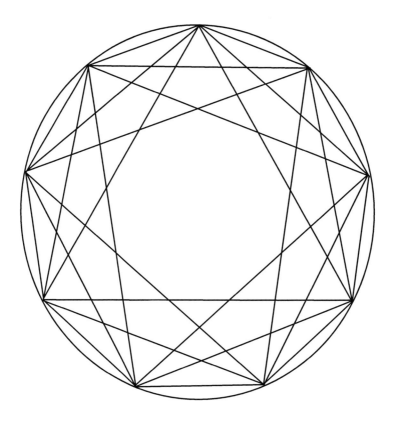

Fig. 11   SEAL OF THE TENTH DIMENSION

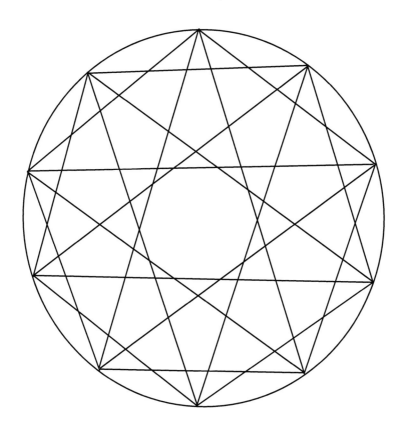

Fig. 12   SEAL OF THE ELEVENTH DIMENSION

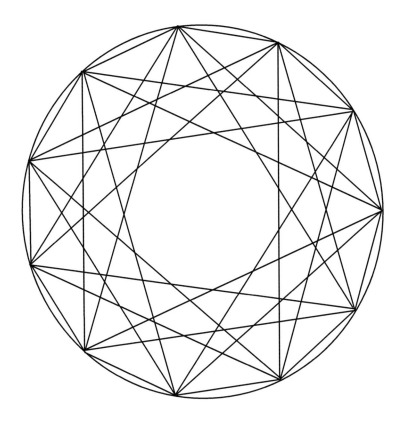

Fig. 13   SEAL OF THE TWELFTH DIMENSION

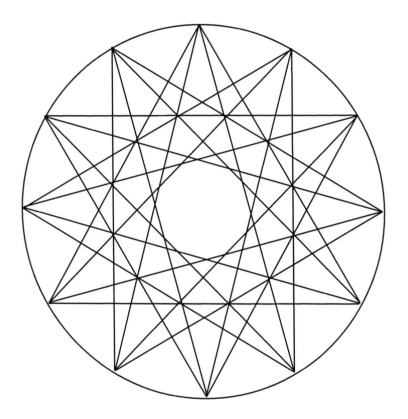

Simply expanding the focus brings consciousness into the experience of each level and the experience of the energies is the teacher of each level. Always keep in mind to take each step of practice slowly. Meditating on the seals opens the doorways in consciousness to prepare for more spiritual responsibility in the creation process.

There are numerous ways to approach the teachings we present. We shall offer further explanation of the seeming paradox between one-pointed focus and the many numbers of multidimensional frequency. Begin by placing your conscious intent upon one ideal and holding this ideal vision of one-pointed focus within the center-point of your conscious awareness. Next carry it to all the points of each seal. When you attain the mastery of holding an ideal in your one-pointed focus and disseminating it into the many dimensions, then your next practice can be to hold more than one ideal in a one-pointed focus directed to the many dimensions. This in itself should stir your consciousness towards further grasp, and it is not our intent to overwhelm those of you not quite prepared for the level of masterful creative power we present to you. We offer you these explanations to stretch your awareness into the power available to create worlds and universes. Now that you see a glimpse into the conscious work of the Master Creator God beings, can you not understand that we tell you all of these things you will do and more? You are the "more" of the equation, for as in the two into one and the three into one, you are the one that is coming into new existence from each dimension accessed. With each dimensional portal you open, you create a multitude of new dimensions. Therefore, we say, "You are the new creation."

Just as you must stretch your physical muscles in the body to gain strength, you must stretch your consciousness or it too will atrophy in its stagnation just like unused muscles. As you impress these images of the sacred seals upon the mind, it will become easier to recall the images to the third eye inwardly without staring at a page. We encourage you once again to play with the esoteric meanings within all words as it will lead you to the purity of the energy vibration at Source. When you gaze upon each seal do you allow yourself to "see all" that each will reveal?

Star Essences

As you activate the energies of the seals you will be aligning your four-body system to the twelve-body chakra system and to the star systems, but you must also ground the energies into the earth consciousness. The use of herbs, aroma essences and other earth elementals have long been an aid to ground the star elements to the earth plane, as well as elevate the consciousness of the earth elements to the stars. Energies are to be transmuted and synthesized through the spiritual human being. Star elements reflect your evolution into the realm of the spiritual human being. Let us clarify further so that your human ego does not misinterpret the energies of creation that we refer to as the star essences with a galactic level of evolution. We in no way infer that the star essences are limited to being associated only with the galactic beings that you refer to as the "space brothers." Qualities of the star essences permeate all levels of creation in this universe from galactic, solar, planetary and into the four kingdoms of your plane. In our use of the term "star essences" we refer to the aspects of energy that are the building blocks of creation inherent within the solar Light. Your sun is a star, and it represents the principles of solar activation and fusion as the center-point of consciousness of your solar system. Star essences are crystallized energy patterns that are of a higher vibratory nature than the elements found on your planet. They also have multidimensional layers of meaning to be revealed. You will discover the nature of these star elements through activating the keys in the inner vision of your "third eye," the eye that is singular. Activating the dimensional seals within your consciousness aligns your level of consciousness with the higher vibratory elements of the star essences or to use another term "solar principles," and this will not only escalate and accelerate your individual alignment process but will also accelerate toward the alignment of the evolutionary process in the body of greater humanity. There is always less room for error in creation when one is in tune harmonically aligned with all systems. We refer to error as being out of tune or out of alignment with the greater rhythm of the cosmic flow of energy in exercising the conscious creative powers.

We can only allude to an overview of the meaning and the power inherent in the star essences herein outlined, as you must learn to experience them through your Higher Self. Each one will intuit the greater understanding of the star roots in your own individual as well as Group Soul awakenings. Many names ring forth the power of the root syllables, and wherever you shall see these syllables you will intuit a greater understanding of the powers of creation that be. Combining the syllables of the star essences become Words of Power. Within the variety of combinations of the star essence syllables will be revealed the attunement with a Higher Purpose. We in no way imply that this list is complete. The star essences listed in the table are just a brief overview of the many components of the creation process for there is always more knowledge to acquire.

As you work to uncover the layers of multidimensional under-standing, you will unlock more of the powers of creation at your command. All of this work is done internally through opening the consciousness to the multidimensional energies within the Heart of the atom, as there is no certainty to comprehend the higher frequencies of this pure intelligence through the limita-tions of the fourth dimension. As the "fallen continuum," fourth dimensional experience is a reflective surface and cannot elicit the level of understanding that is gleaned through direct ex-perience of the pure Light of intelligent self-awareness at the Heart of the matter. (The pronounciation of the "a" vowel in all syllables is pronounced with a "short a" sound as in "ah.")

STAR ROOT SYLLABLE	STAR ESSENCE	DOMAIN OF POWER	INTENT OF COMMAND
AH	Inspiration	Etheric Breath	Spirit breaths new life into the form of creation
AN	Coalescence	Power of One-pointed Focus	Holding the con-sciousness without waver upon the ideal form
AL	Invocation	Power to Command	Calling forth The Word of creation
AR	Synergy	Synthesis of Energies	Alchemy of the two into one
AT	Evolution	Power to Become	The new creation of the two into one, the three into one, and so forth into infinity through eternity

AZ	Effusion	Power of The Word upon the Waters of Life	Bringing forth the essence of the re-fined ideal through thought and deed
BA	Devotion	The Light upon Peaceful Waters	Steadiness of the Mind upon the Heart
DO	Intonation	Activation of Energetic Fields	Attunement to the Divine Breath at Source
EM	Emanation	Power of The Word upon the Creation Fields	Divine Breath issues forth into the many fields of creation
EL	Effulgence	Creator Source Idealized Vision	Pure vision as the State of Being prior to creation
EN	Immanence	Medium of Creation Field	Self-sustaining and self-generating energy without end
HAT	Quickening	Direct Path of Energies	The Cosmic intent radiates a direct path of energies into the manifestation fields
KA	Initiation	Activation of Life Energies	The stirring towards the quickening and awakening of evolution
KU	Provenance	The Will to Direct Energies	Focus of Will to direct energies upon the manifestation field

MA	Unification	Medium of Manifestation Field	Merging the dimensional fields of manifestation
MER	Equilibration	Balance of Opposing Forces	Attainment of the center-point of balancing the opposing forces through the powerful steadiness of intent
NA	Edification	Power of The Word upon the Manifestation Field	Wisdom Teachings of the Ages that always were and those yet to come
OM	Revelation	Trinity of Completion	The Omnipresence of the Masterful One. What goes forth must return threefold and hence to go forth again in multitude
ON	Reflection	Mediation of Energies, Principalities	The Creator beholds the Light reflecting upon the dark waters
OO	Harmonic	The Symphony of the Spheres	Octaves within octaves of sound creation
OR	Pulsation	Governance of Cycles	The pause between the inhalation and exhalation of Divine Breath through all multidimensional spheres
RA	Radiance	Solar Activation, Light Infusion	Adding Light to the Light that is already

SOL	Illumination	Bringing Forth Light	Ignites from within
TAH	Synthesis	Fusion of Light and Matter	Transfiguration of matter through refinement

Although the use of fourth-dimensional language made in the reference to manifestation fields and creation fields may appear as if it is the same energetic frequency, they are different bandwidths of energetic vibration. The term "manifestation fields" refers to localized spheres of creation, whereas reference to the term "creation fields" is the eternal and infinite Cosmic creation. We beseech you again to not let the small mindedness of the ego aspect of your consciousness limit your understandings. We herein allude to merely the primary basics of these powerful essences at the heart of the creation principle. Always and a day remember that each name of power and each syllable on the breath of being is layered with multidimensional meaning. Nothing is as limiting in the Cosmos as that of the distortion of the ego interpretations within the fourth dimensional frequencies. The intent of Words of Power upon the creation fields bring forth your existence, as you bring forth the existence of infinity.

STAR ESSENCE GLOSSARY	
AH – OO – EM:	(Aum) The I AM of masterful creation
AL – AH:	Almighty power of the Divine Breath into the pure energies of the living creation
AN – KA – RA:	The power of one-pointed focus to activate the energies of evolution through Light Infusion

AN – OO:	The power of one-pointed focus of harmonic frequency
AN – TAH – KA – RA – NA:	The power of one-pointed focus to infuse Light into matter and coalesce into form. The ongoing process of awakening of the God Creator being through initiation and direct connection with Source energy. Setting forth The Word of manifestation.
AN – TAH – RA:	Primary steps of one-pointed focus to infuse Light into matter to build the Antahkarana
AT – EN:	Eternal evolution through the infinity of the creation fields
AT – OM:	The one that is more than the sum of its parts omnipresent through the manifestation fields
AT – ON:	Sets the tone of evolution distributed from the thrones and principalities. Dispensation of energies to appropriate levels of energetic frequencies throughout the universes
AZ – RA – EL:	Thou shall bring forth the Word upon the waters of manifestation through the refined essences of joy
BA – AL:	Power to command the Light upon the peaceful waters. You shall walk in Peace and be the reflection of the peaceful waters.
DO – RA – EL:	Solar Light returns threefold upon the waves of resonant creation
EN – KU - AN:	Pure focus of will throughout the creation cycles

EN – RA – EL:	Regeneration of the Light infused into the matter worlds to redirect towards the perfection of the Ideal
KU – MA – RA:	The Will to direct the energies of creation across the manifestation fields to infuse the Light of intelligent awareness, thus ensuring the evolution process.
MA – AT:	The power to become is the evolution of unification. The creation born of the unification of two becomes more than the two through evolution.
MA – HAT – MA:	The Cosmic intent radiates the direct path of energies into the denser manifestation fields to instigate the quickening.
MER – KA – BA:	Awakening to the evolution which brings about the balance of opposing forces and the steadiness of the mind upon the Heart
NA – AL:	From out of The Word of the Language of Light comes the ever new creation
RA – MA - AT:	Evolution of unification through Light infusion
SOL – AR:	Synthesizing the energies of the Light brought forth through the new creation. You are the solution.
SOL – OM – ON:	Ignited from within the Masterful One the Light goes forth to shine upon the darkness and the truth is revealed

At each level of dimensional vibration the "power word" or "name" elicits varying levels of powerful command. We offer you here a sample of some very powerful star root syllables.

There are the many names within the nameless, and we are not inclined to address the impossible with any attempt to attain the infinitude of the multitude within a few brief paragraphs. However, let us offer a bit of further explanation in brevity about the *ELOHIM*. The EL (idealized vision) -OH (of) -IM (I AM) is the idealized vision of the "I AM." Many more layers of meaning are to be found within this most potent and powerful name of command used by the Master Creator God beings that sit upon the thrones at the threshold of the Holy of Holies. This is only one of their many roles within the carrying forth of Divine Plan into the Cosmic creation fields. Divine Love ever and a day will find a new way to express the heights and depths of its beautiful array.

Synthesizing the triad of the earth consciousness and the star consciousness into the emerging spiritual human being is the core essence of the work to be done. The spiritual human being stands upon the threshold of unification and now steps more fully into the powerful command of the I AM presence of mastery.

There is a trinity or threefold factor to the merging of Gaia earth consciousness, the spiritual human being and the star essence. There are those doing work with Gaia consciousness. They are sometimes referred to as the earth-keepers and tribal people. Then there are those working with the star consciousness sometimes referred to as the starry beings. All these paths lead towards unification. However, it is truly the path of the spiritual human being to straddle the thresholds of both the earth and the stars. The earth is one factor, the stars are another factor, but the spiritual human being that accomplishes bringing these two elements in unification is the third factor completing the trinity of the creation process at this next level of evolution.

The spiritual human being is the third key in the trinity that be-comes the portal itself to other dimensions. The spiritual human being . As the center-point of balance literally between the vi-bratory realms of heaven's stars and earth's firmament, the spiri-tual human being is the merging point of this field of creation. Be mindful that this is only one level of explanation of the trinity of creation. Creation in its very primary basics is a threefold process, and therein is the understanding of why your religious books have referred to "the holy trinity." Advanced complexities of creation exist beyond the basic three-fold formula for there are dimensions within dimensions ad infinitum.

In the beginning stages of the new creation, there will still be those that will do the bodywork and the acupuncture for there are overlapping levels of the evolutionary awaken-ings, but there are those that will bring in the new healing lev-els of energy transference. This work is aligned with telepathic rapport and conscious utilization of the star essence qualities. Telepathic rapport begins with opening to your own Higher Consciousness and working in coordination with the Ascended Host. Although some have already tapped into and are utilizing some of the basics of this alignment process with distance heal-ing techniques and grounding the Light, we refer to the trans-ference of this energy to another being or to the earth sphere as an entirely new level of communication and healing not yet utilized on your plane. Distance healing and activating the Light matrix grids have been the preliminary level of the next phase shift of this conscious evolvement. This telepathic rapport is es-sentially what we do with you. We are teaching you to be as we are. We are teaching you to be the Masters that we know you to be. To speak of being the teacher does not negate you to some underling level of forever remaining the student. Perception of the One in relationship to all its aspects is forever the goal of awakening your consciousness. A Master teaches mastery by being masterful. A student learns to be masterful by awakening the Master within. We, the Ascended Host, are but the mirror of your own becoming, and we see in your reflection that you are becoming.

Once again we remind you to tarry not your attention on the titles of the tasks to be accomplished, for many of you embody multiple traits and accomplish multiple tasks. We offer you merely guidelines to use as tools along your way. Each and every worker in the Light must eventually work with all of the elements of creation. Do not be concerned with categories and linear type thinking. You are the multidimensional awakened ones, so be not surprised by the extent of your own multi-talents. Many of you will perform more than one task or harness more than one star essence in your efforts and may discover that you are able to perform them simultaneously. Many of you will awaken more traits as you apply yourselves to the tasks at hand. You will also take note that many of you have set up extreme challenges on your path to overcome as a test of your own spiritual fortitude. We gently remind you that you are already powerful and testing your stamina and resilience is not necessary. You are all free to release these challenges in any instantaneous moment that you so empower yourself with this choice. Remind yourself of the ease and elegance that is your spiritual birthright. The power of creation is yours to command.

The most important discipline on the path to mastery is the discipline of the ego. Its little voice must be silenced in order for the powerful and commanding voice of the Higher Self to prevail. You are much vaster than your ego would allow you to accept. The limiting and negative voice of the ego is the ultimate trickster. Be ever vigilant not to fall for its tricks. It is the ultimate deceiver of the truth of your magnificence. Catch it in its act of deception. Stop it in its tracks and shift your consciousness to the empowerment of the Higher Self. You must stand guard against your own ego, while also rising above all external situations steeped in embittered ego battles. Your only goal and whole-hearted focus must be to fulfill the carrying forth of Divine Plan. Unity is the key word to remember. Focus must be directed on unification as the underlying basis of all actions set forth. Unification implies many levels. We speak of the unification of the earth body to awaken to the physical body, the physical body to awaken to the spiritual body, and the spiritual body to awaken to the galactic body. There are layers within layers for we speak of each cell to awaken to the human body, each Soul to awaken to Group Soul, and each sun to awaken to its galaxy.

Divine Plan is complex in its nature for it spans eons. Hence you must not hesitate to understand the necessity to bridge the multidimensional spheres of consciousness in order to reintegrate the fallen continuum of your world in realignment attuned to the greater cosmic rhythm. We have explained that a portion of consciousness has fallen into unconsciousness. We have also explained that "the fall" refers to the dense vibration of fear generated from the unconscious and creating fearful images in the fourth dimension. Humanity has fallen out of rhythm with the cosmos, and you have heard this called by many terms. References have been made to the fallen continuum, the unconscious realm, earth rising, the ascension, the next quantum leap, the Great Shift, the Golden Age and much more. The worker in the Light is aware of the focus to raise the resonance, to heal and balance the emotional energies and unblock the energies of the chakras, and to align with Higher Consciousness. These activities are all part of the process, but there is so much more you have yet to awaken.

A worker poised on the threshold of eternity is of valuable service to the task of integrating the dimensional frequencies. Do not hesitate to straddle that threshold. Many are needed to hold the balance between the realms.

We of the Ascended Host are the Master designers of the blueprints of Divine Plan. You are the builders of the cities of Light. Together with our combined efforts we are the architects of Light. There is naught the Ascended Host can accomplish without the cooperative efforts of the workers in the Light on earth. The legions of Light in the higher vibratory realms are mighty in force, but your power is mightier still. You are both the road traveled and the map. You are both the Master mason and the temple. You are the creator awakening within its creation. Do not underestimate the power you have to transform your world. The combined efforts of all those aligned with Divine Plan assures that the outcome is already guaranteed. This does not mean that the workers in the Light can rest on their laurels. The Great Work awaits you, and there are many tasks to accomplish. In truth, the Great Work is never finished for evolution is everlasting. During this period of accelerated frequencies, we put forth the effort to work with you in fulfillment of this phase of Divine Plan. Take to heart these very words at the heart of the truth that evolution is expansion of consciousness and a refinement of energies. Reach and stretch your awareness with us. Reach for the stars for you are the stars, and you will arrive at home with another aspect of your Self. Do not halt there, as the galaxy awaits you. Just at the edge of your imagination, there is always more. The road within is the only road that leads home. Enter into the portal of the Heart of Hearts within and find yourself warmed by the home fires in the Great Central Sun. From out of the Great Central Sun emanates the multitude of suns. What goes forth must return threefold and hence to go forth again in multitude.

A Master plan is the accomplishment of mastery over the many multidimensional levels of conscious creation in unification to bring forth the manifestation of idealized vision. You are the blueprints and the template of your future Self. You are both creator and created. You are the design that is Divine.

THREE

TEMPLES OF THE SOUL

*In the center is the eternal flame,
and its Light is seen by few.*

Each soul is unique. Each soul uniquely reflects the Divine. Each individuated soul is on the path of separation during involution/descension. Each individuated soul is on the path of unification during evolution/ascension. With each step taken downward, there is a step taken upward simultaneously. Ascension is not an ending, just as descension is not a beginning. They are but two aspects of the One in rhythmic pulsation manifesting throughout the creation fields.

The human body is the Temple of the Soul. Creation of the cities of Light begins with the creation of the temple. The human body is the master template of the temple. Break down the word template into the anagram *"at temple."* Consciousness housed within the body is already "at temple." There is no real need to travel anywhere, but in the new creation, external temples will be built to align with the template of the body that houses the Soul in attunement with the new earth grid matrix. Energies of the Group Soul will align with the temple in manifestation. Building of the Temples of the Soul is yet another aspect of Divine Plan in the externalization of the Kingdom. Characteristics embodied in the spiritual human being will determine the construction of the external temples. Returning to the sacred sanctity of honoring the Soul is at hand. This is the return of the Divine Feminine that has been the proclamation of many prophets, and it is returning through the expression and honoring of the Soul. The external Temples of the Soul will be places of Group Soul gathering, places of teaching and spiritual study and places of meditation honoring and allowing the state of being that is the landscape of the Soul. Schools of the higher sciences of the creation principle will be a core focus of teaching in the temples. Each Soul will gravitate to their individual level of accessing and gaining more spiritual power, truth, knowledge and wisdom. Crystal clarity generation of one-pointed focus will be a mainstay. Festivities and communal celebrations will be held in the gardens of the temple grounds. There will be no priests or leaders, for all will participate in unified purpose. Each one has gifts to contribute and areas of teachings to bring forth to share. Each one will continue to work towards evolvement and, by doing so, will add to the awakening knowledge of consciousness and add to the Group Soul. Concurrent with the theme of unification through telepathic rapport, each will know which tasks to fulfill and will go about fulfilling them. Each unique Soul has a place to fill that no other can fill. There will still be some who are not yet prepared for telepathic rapport. Other levels of teaching and learning to bring forth unification will need to be employed. The Temple of the Soul will be both the awakening to the body as the temple, which is consciousness in constant movement, and also alignment with the stationary temples of Group Soul gatherings along the ascended earth grid matrix.

Prime in the example to be set through Group Soul effort is the value bestowed on each and every human being born into the world to be deemed precious and offered the greatest dignity rightful of each heir to the kingdom. As a ruby glows red and an emerald shines green in its luster so too does each child brought forth into manifestation shine the Golden and Silver halo of prime Source Light.

In generalized principle, your sun is one of many manifestations of the temple of the Spirit. Ignite the eternal flame at the center of your body temple, and likewise unify with the flame at the core of the earth and the solar fire of your sun. In this way, the human Soul is fused with the earth Soul and weds the Soul to the Spirit that is the Light of the solar aspect bringing forth the sacred marriage often referred to as "heaven on earth." All of these principles permeate each dimension and inclusion is key to understanding expansion of consciousness. Beginning in the Temple of the Soul of the human being when the solar fire of the Spirit is ignited in the Heart of Hearts, this unification of Spirit and Soul is the sacred marriage within the Higher Self. As this flame burns in the human temple, it ignites the earth and sun to fuse also in the sacred marriage, as all is unified at Divine Source. From out of the flame of Source through the temples of creation emanates the spiritual essences of the Soul. Oh ye keepers of the flame keep the flame burning.

As in every stage of the initial construction of the new creation, the blueprints of the Temple of the Soul begin once again with the foundation. A foundation is a state of being. Upon the foundation the temple is built. The foundation is the embodiment in the spiritual human being of higher resonating frequencies aligned with spiritual principles and ethics. The temple component is the essence of the Higher Self. As each awakening spiritual human being embodies more and more of the traits of the foundation, this allows for the Higher Self to merge the higher essences of each trait in unification. In this way the Temple of the Soul is built within the human vehicle to house the Spirit and unify the two into the one that is referred to as the Higher Self.

There have been many questions posed regarding the Higher Self. Is it just one Higher Self or many Higher Selves of each individuated Soul? Once more we bring your attention to the truth that all in creation is number. Within the One is the infinity of number that has no end. Revisiting the teachings of the two into one and the three into one, we shall say that the same applies. Within each individuated Soul wedded to the Spirit housed in the bodily temple of the spiritual human being, this creates the two into one, and therefore, creates a new entity in the same manner that the split into duality creates the trinity or the third entity of creation. Each of you are literally birthing your Higher Self as the third entity when you wed your Soul and Spirit, just as you are birthed from out of your Higher Self in the split of duality within the One during the creation process. It is a two-way street of the exhalation and inhalation of creation. As Divine Breath splits itself into duality to exhale into the manifested fields of creation, and inhales on its return merging of the two into one, this does not mean that all returns to a state of dissolving back into the oneness prior to creation. The apparent folly in that should be obvious. What in truth it does imply is that "one more" or another new aspect of the One is now created within the One, and thus the One is continuously expanding. Paradox knocks upon your door once more. When those moments where creation may appear meaningless also knock upon your door, understand that creation brings meaning to conscious awakening at the individuated as well as collective Soul level. If only you will allow just a fragment of understanding the beauty of this endless sea of infinite creation through eternity, awe would become your natural state of awareness.

What is the foundation of the state of being and the temple components to build upon we refer to? The Soul seeks expression of the intangible qualities of spiritual essence through the Spirit made manifest. Within the blueprints of the new creation, it is necessary to begin manifesting through an entirely new foundation of spiritual essence than previous creations in your planetary scheme. This is a simple formula for the twelve into one and the creation of the twenty-four.

4 Cornerstones + 4 Pillars + 4 Inner Temple = 12 x 2 = 24

FOUNDATION	TEMPLE COMPONENT
CORNERSTONES	
Grace	Divinity
Integrity	Dignity
Gratitude	Honor
Intuition	Telepathy
PILLARS	
Kindness	Compassion
Knowledge	Wisdom
Clarity	Truth
Amazement	Wonder
INNER TEMPLE	
Joy	Ecstasy
Harmony	Serenity
Tranquility	Peace
Faith	Trust
CENTER	
Eternal Flame of the Light of Divine Source	

Each component of the temple floor plan is constructed with dual counterparts of the higher essence along with its offspring. What is the spiritual essence of anything but that which is essential? This design of the blueprints of the Temple of the Soul is to ensure balance in the merging of the higher resonating dimensions with the lower resonating dimensions.

Divinity/Grace, Dignity/Integrity, Honor/Gratitude, and Telepathy/Intuition are the cornerstones of the temple. Returning to the state of grace is to accept one's divinity. By existing in the state of grace, one allows the embodiment of its higher essence of Divinity. Integrity is the basis of dignity. Each action based on spiritual integrity creates the space for more human dignity. Gratitude bestows honor and in return begets more gratitude to yet make way to bestow more honor. Intuition is a key to unlock the door to telepathy. As more trust is placed in the intuition, the door to telepathy swings open wider.

Compassion/Kindness is one pillar of support in the foundation of the temples of the new creation. Wisdom/Knowledge, Truth/Clarity, Wonder/Amazement are the other pillars. Kindness is the offspring of empathy. Compassion is its higher essence. Kindness begins with a simple act towards another and evolves into compassion that embraces and encompasses the all of the creation fields. Knowledge is born from awareness. Wisdom is its higher essence. Knowledge is infinite and perpetual and evolves into wisdom when it is applied to all facets of creation. Clarity is born from discernment. Truth is its higher essence. Clarity arrives when truth surfaces through the muddied emotional waters from the infinitely pure depths of the Soul. Amazement is born from innocence. Wonder is its higher essence. Amazement stands witness to each act of creation. Wonder is the state of awe from out of which innocence is born anew.

The four rooms of the inner temple are Ecstasy/Joy, Se-

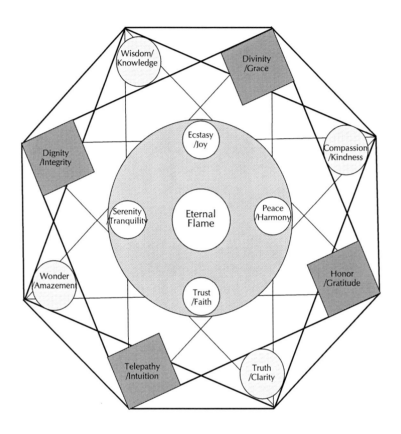

Fig. #14   TEMPLE OF THE SOUL

renity/Tranquility, Peace/Harmony and Trust/Faith. Rippling waves of joy prepare the way for the experience of ecstasy. Harmony must be created to ensure peace. The key component to peace is harmony in all things. Harmony resonates when each one refines the thoughts and emotions to its higher essence. Tranquility must be attained first before seeking the center of serenity. When the Heart is tranquil then serenity is its home. One must stand upon the rock of faith in order to trust that which is beyond grasp. Faith is the prelude to trust. Faith is exercised, as trust is the arrival point of its destination.

The kingdom within is first built upon these foundations. These are the days of the externalization of the kingdom. We have said that Light is intelligent awareness, and we will remind you again. Thinking, reasoning and comprehension are functions of intelligence. Awareness is the state of being conscious. Consciousness uses the faculty of thinking inherent in its intelligence, while intuition is in the territory of awareness. We have said that wisdom is a component of Divine Love. Wisdom is intelligent awareness that has evolved into the highest state of the pure awareness of knowing. Wisdom applied is the kingdom gained.

There is a fine line of distinction between the "knowing it is so" of mastery over giving the ego a platform for its arrogance of "thinking it knows." To give these spirtual explanations of the truth to the level of the ego is again how the distortion becomes manifest on your plane.

Embodying these spiritual essentials is the foundation of your state of being in the many worlds within worlds. Even embodied in their least expression, they are qualities far more healing and far-reaching than all the present therapy modalities being utilized. Embodied in their fullest degree such power of

Divine Love unleashed would bring all Souls directly home to the Heart of Hearts of the matter. We have said that a foundation is merely a resting place to teach you that all foundations are temporary states of being. When the conscious mind gets attached to any foundation, it is time to loosen its grip and step into the flexibility that consciousness is in reality. We in no way imply that your state of consciousness should be indecisive or scattered in many directions. The masterful conscious one must stand firm on the intangible foundations of ethics, principles and absolute faith and put forth intent without waver. When the feat is accomplished then consciousness must expand into ever-new manifestation fields. This calls for expanding the horizons of the foundations at each level of awakening to power. In accord with this truth, understand that ever beyond each new foundation of being there is always infinity for consciousness to expand into and eternity to harness the powers of creation to express newer foundations of consciousness.

The example template of the Soul diagram is a sample of many such temples that can be built. This is not to put limitation on the layout of any form but simply used as a guideline sample of what is possible to construct both within the inner kingdom and the externalization of the kingdom on the basis of sacred geometry. Always and a day let the higher intuition lead the way.

Future unfolding visions impart that any and all manifestation in the new dimensional frequencies will be founded upon the principles of sacred geometry as well as aligned with the meridians and activation points of Light. Whereas in the historical times of your planet the designers and architects used their imagination and creativity to build structures that were not aligned with the principles of sacred geometry, all future endeavors must be in accord with these principles. A greater understanding of this will be revealed in the alignment of the temple layouts with the template on the etheric level, and this attunement will bring forth greater harmony than you can yet grasp with your most vivid imagination. With the acceleration of intense frequency vibrations, the old thought patterns that created in the old paradigm will not sustain the new level of your thought vibrations, and most especially these spiritual traits of joy, ecstasy, truth and so on, cannot be housed in anything unlike itself. As in the example of the pyramids, structures built upon the principles of sacred geometry are designed for longevity. Ordinary structures crumble in a period of much shorter intervals. Although we repeat that all form is temporal and, therefore, temporary, the scientific principles of sacred geometry are aligned with what have often been referred to as the immortal realms. Even the immortal realms are not immortal in the sense of form being preserved for eternity, for all form shifts and changes as consciousness evolves and shifts focus. More advanced technologies based on sacred geometry exist beyond these presented here, and everyone eventually graduates to the levels of their grasp and comprehension and the ability to apply the knowledge to conscious creation.

As there is the Temple of the Soul in honor of the Divine Feminine so is there the Temple of the Spirit of the Divine Masculine. Whereas the Temple of the Soul is based upon the foundations of the intangible essences of refined states of being, the Temple of the Spirit is associated with the solar principle of harnessing energy and directing it through conscious acts of powerful creation. Energy is self-generating and self-perpetuating. Energy is raw power. The Soul is the passive state of being kind, being full of grace, being compassionate, being truthful, being wise, being serene, being peaceful, being full of wonder, and so on. These energies of the Soul emanate from the center point of balance in their purest and rarefied fundamental nature. The Spirit is the active and dynamic Light that is intelligent consciousness. The energy of the Spirit is power that directs energy by conscious intent. Energy is vibration. Raising the resonant vibration to the intangible qualities of the Soul is primary to then secondarily direct the energy to new heights and levels of manifesting from these new foundations.

The Temple of the Spirit that we refer to is based on a very potent and primal facet of energy at Source. This is not a temple that is manifested in your plane at any time and is only accessed within. There comes a point in the course of spiritual mastery when you will work directly with these energies, which we will also refer to as the Temple of Light, although there are other ancient names that have been bestowed upon it. This is in accord with activating the seventh seal of dimensional creation, although keep in mind each seal has more dimensional frequencies involved beyond your comprehension. Do not be overly concerned with comprehending the entirety of the multi-dimensional Cosmos, but rather always aim to work at the level of your conscious ability to expand in steps and stages.

We begin an introduction for you with the basic geometry of the pyramid. Within the depths of conscious meditation you shall come upon seven pillars of Light surrounding a central pillar of Light. This is the seven into one and the eight of infinity. Do not confuse this as the threshold of the Source, but merely one of many plateaus in the fields of creation. Each of the seven pillars consists of a band of Light frequency, which transmits varying aspects of knowledge. As in any library, when you walk to a certain section to look for certain volumes on a particular subject, you simply approach one of the seven pillars that transmits the branch of knowledge that you seek. These pillars of Light are so powerful that only when one comprehends each of them to a certain degree can the center pillar even be approached. The center pillar is the formula of the seven into one and the infinity of the numerical eight. Within the center pillar are all seven surrounding pillars of knowledge merged. Extreme caution must be exercised in working with these energies to assure that a Master guide is with you before you approach. The Master guide will ground your energies and stabilize them as you work with the pillars of Light, otherwise, the intensity of the energy of this direct knowledge will overwhelm you to the far extremes of emotional, physical, psychological and spiritual unbalance.

Herein is a further explanation. The singular pillar of Light at the center reflects and refracts its Light through seven pyramids. The seven pyramids in turn reflect and refract the Light. Now, if you will understand that to down step these potent energies of the seven pillars through the reflection and refraction process of many levels they become fragmented or refracted into color bands of varying degrees of prismatic reflection. On the fourth dimensional level, prismatic refraction occurs within the sacred geometrical form of the four-sided pyramid and the reflection occurs in each plane. To understand this refraction and reflection, imagine the geometry of the pyramid and at the apex imagine the white Light entering that point. As the Light of the one pointed focus of consciousness enters at the apex, it refracts into the four faces of the pyramidal geometry known as planes or kingdoms thus creating the fourth dimensional manifestation field. The base of the pyramidal geometry is the foundation. The apex of the pyramid represents the heavenly eye that is singular and the foundation represents the earth in this sacred marriage of the energies of creation. This is a simplified explanation of sacred geometry occurring in many levels of complexities of the creation principle. When the reflection and refraction process reaches the dimensional level of creation on your plane this creates the varying chakras of the body systems, including the planets, and the many manifestation fields in your local universe. Each chakra is a mind or a portal to certain aspects of knowledge.* Mind centers of the chakra systems permeate the manifestation and creation fields. Perhaps you can better understand how the age old art of astrology associates the planets with certain aspects of energies and specific or particular aspects of knowledge. There are actually twelve planets in your particular solar system, which correlate to the twelve-chakra system. Just as the chakras in the body each disseminate a function of its own mind aligned with the combined mind of all seven chakras, so too do the planets embody and disseminate functions of energies combined within the one solar temple of the sun. The planets are the chakras of the solar system, which exists within the greater galactic body and so forth. Within each layer of bodies is the connection to Divine Love at Source through the Heart of Hearts. Your solar sun is the Heart of Hearts chakra of your solar system at that level of consciousness. Once again, we assure you that this is a simplified explanation of the reality of this process of the emanations of the eternal and infinite Light across the creation fields. The seven-chakra system within the body is but the primary beginnings of understanding this system of seven. The twelve-chakra system houses the seven-chakra system and is based in a greater understanding of these principles ampli

---

* For more information on the twelve-chakra system, see *The Rhythm of the Cosmic Pulse,* pp 106-111.

fied exponentially. If you expand your comprehension to understand that the Temple of Light matrix and the seven into one is the template blueprint for the seven-chakra system of transforming the Light of knowledge into the physical plane of matter, some understanding may be comprehended at your level of conscious evolution. Again we reference your attention that the Temples of Light are only accessed within through the meditation process. Accessing the Divine Source of Light must always be done through a balance of the Spirit/Soul within the center of the Heart of Hearts. We remind you again that this level of the seven pillars of Light merging into the eighth or central pillar is not the threshold of Divine Source, but just one of many beginning entry levels towards advancement.

Towards the idealized goal of the new creation building of the Temples of the Soul begins within in the state of being before it can be externalized in the outer manifestation process. Embodiment of the high ideals and refined essences of spiritual qualities must be the goal towards which to reach attainment. With each essence of the Soul awakened in portions will each Spirit express its Light of the essence into the fields of manifestation. Esoterically speaking, from within the center flame of the Temple of the Soul, the Light pillars of the temple of the Spirit are activated and sent forth through the focus of one-pointed consciousness into manifestation. The expression of the Temple of the Soul through the Temple of the Spirit is another aspect of the sacred marrige of the Higher Self that is becoming the heaven on earth template.

Just as the human body is the Temple of the Soul, the earth is your temple ground. Plant your gardens as idealized thought made manifest on the temple grounds. Nurture your gardens from the wellsprings of your inner beauty. Celebrate beauty. Beauty is not glamour. Glamour fades along the corridors of linear time. Beauty is eternal. Glamour shimmers briefly on the surface of ever changing tides. Beauty can only be found in the depths of the Soul. Glamour is a by-product from the erosion of high ideals. Beauty is the embodiment of high ideals.

For too long the Soul has been cast to the shadows of consciousness and thus we shift your focus towards the reconnection with this most wondrous landscape of the Divine Feminine. Through the silencing of the Soul's voice, the land has become arid, and imagination has become like the desert wilderness in the histories of your times. For too long the animation of the Spirit has been given over to the ego's clamoring voice as the driving force in the histories of your times. Fifth dimensional frequencies are available to lift each one and all of humanity out of the revolving door of history when each individual is ready to ascend on the wings of their own uplifting. Fifth dimensional energies of unlimited imagination to utilize in bringing forth the new creation will reveal to you just how much experience of your consciousness has been confined to the fourth dimensional existence your ego clings to. Awakening to the individual Soul will open the door to the infinity of the World Soul and thus the Universal Soul and ultimately the Cosmic Soul of the Divine Feminine in expression through the Divine Masculine Spirit.

Upon the sacred temple grounds the Soul walks hand in hand with the Spirit in expression of the beauty made manifest in the new creation. This dance can in no way be rivaled in any corner of your current fourth dimensional world of repeating history. Lift ye up the voice of the Soul and sing its song to herald the new creation for yet there is still more and more is yet to be.

FOUR

AWAKENING THE GROUP SOUL

Synergy is the key to group harmony.

There are many trinities within the patterns of conscious creation. Just as consciousness awakens at the three levels of the personal, global and universal levels of awareness all merging into the consciousness of the Higher Self, so it is with the Soul awakening. The Soul awakens on the personal level. It awakens on the global level referred to as the anima mundi, and it also awakens to the universal level, which is what we will herein refer to as Group Soul. Group Soul effort is of the universal scheme of Divine Plan, which in turn brings the vision into manifestation on your earth plane. As in all such awakenings of consciousness, there is no set pattern or linear movement. There simply is the attunement to the various levels of consciousness. Consciousness shifts focus. Consciousness expands or contracts its focus.

Seeds of the potential for Group Soul effort have been placed in the soil of consciousness by the Master Creator God beings in what could be considered from your vantage point of linear history as times past. Future potential was engrafted on the human DNA. We are watching the seeds now breaking through the soil in what could be considered your time of the present. Some buds have already blossomed, and the fruits of some Group Soul effort have already ripened on the vine. There will be many more vineyards and many more beautiful gardens of the Soul to grow. Manifestation through creation and evolution in accord with Divine Plan is a process, which from your perspective appears linear but from our perspective in reality is exponential expansion and contraction of the rhythmic pulsation of the Divine Breath. From our view, we perceive you as multidimensional layers of potential overlaying the perfected template. In essence, you were all birthed with the seeds of universal potential intact. However, there are points of your conscious awakening throughout the multidimensional spheres of manifestation that trigger the effects of the evolutionary process. Your Higher Self instigates you to awaken to these trigger points of potential, and this is termed as the thresholds of initiation. Once they are awakened, activation of certain codes already inherent in the DNA set in effect the next evolutionary leaps. This is what we refer to as seeds placed in the soil. DNA functions like the memory in a computer chip but is also much more than that. It is a calculator in a certain sense also for its basis of function is numerical, and you must take into consideration that alphabet sequencing is also based in number. Seeds of evolution are programmed into the DNA and when activated through the merging of the conscious and Higher Conscious intent, the DNA is impressed with new programming. Pre-encoded numerical formulas set into motion the multidimensional frequencies of vibration within each cell. Divine Plan is open ended, and by this we mean that the DNA is updated and reprogrammed concordant with certain levels of attainment. Evolutionary Divine Plan is dependent on your conscious participation to open to the levels of your Higher Consciousness to activate the pre-encoded programming, as well as to impress it with new programming.

Similar to the binary system of ones and zeroes in your computers the human DNA has a far more complex numbering system, which allows for the imprinting of new data to stretch into infinite proportions. Within the components of your desktop computer programming you are aware that you run out of memory and storage space with limitations on how many programs can be running at the same time. Proportionate to the numerical formula in the DNA, programming has more far-reaching and multidimensional potential. Reprogramming of the DNA does not occur without the effect of consciousness upon it but remains dormant until such time of its conscious activation. Continuing with the computer metaphor, by this we mean as the Higher Self instigates the awakening of the evolutionary program, the conscious mind must now download the new programming and learn to run this program. In this way the conscious mind becomes more of the Higher Conscious mind and directs intent into the local manifestation fields from a more expanded aspect of consciousness. Human DNA is programmed and updated accordingly to create the temple form of consciousness that is to be the library of the Language of Light. As a living library of the Language of Light, the awakened spiritual human is in its evolutionary state of becoming the central point of communication connector throughout a multitude of multidimensional spheres of consciousness. This is why we say you are the design that is Divine. From the clay of the earth you were born, but on the wings in formation of the dove to the stars you will return.

Phase shifts created from the greater rhythm of the cosmic pulse ripple through the multidimensional realms opening the portals to instigate great shifts in the consciousness of humanity. Phase shifts are energetic instigators of conscious intent from the Ascended Host, or to put it in simpler terms a bit of a

Cosmic nudge to stir up activity in your dimensions. From the threshold of the Elohim, conscious intent of visionary implications are impressed upon the energetic ripples of frequency vibration. These phase shifts ripple as the rhythmic beat of the Heart of Hearts through the multidimensional layers of this creation plan to ultimately reach to the fifth, sixth and seventh dimensional spheres. Consciousness impresses consciousness, which imprints the DNA with new information. From the energy of the fifth, sixth and seventh dimensional spheres, the workers in the Light must consciously harness the energy through grounding it in the human vehicle infusing the higher resonating energies into the fourth dimension. The density of the fourth dimension is then uplifted through refinement to the heights of the fifth and so forth. Transmutation occurs through this process, and small portions of the fourth dimensional frequencies are merged through ascension into the fifth dimensional sphere of consciousness. The transmuted portions are herein sometimes referred to as "pockets of Light" in reference to the stages of the ascension process on your plane. It is why you witness some people holding their center balance point within the Light, while at the same time eruptions of fearful chaos litter the landscape around them. Each step of transmutation then shifts the dimensions into an elevated state of resonance towards more harmony. Resistance to the phase shift injections of energy can be more disruptive than productive due to the levels of fear being emphasized. Fear is the greatest inhibitor to the birth of the Golden Age. Like a mother tensing during the birth contractions inhibits the baby from entering the world more peacefully, so it is when those who are to birth the new creation tense up in their fear of such a grand and joyous event. As each individual merges the dimensions consciously, it brings more of the fallen continuum into resonant harmony with Source. This is the explanation you seek when wondering if your world is not appearing to literally be splitting in two. Re-emphasis is needed to say that all depends on the workers in the Light to achieve the transmutation process in order for the greater portion of your plane to be able to ascend. Any energy that is unlike the increased vibrations cannot move into the next phase. Therefore, fear based realities can not and will not exist in the new creation. Free choice reigns supreme as to which vibration any individual chooses to exist within. As more of the workers in Light hold the resonance attuned to the higher frequencies consistently, those that cling to fear will be faced with the choice to attune their consciousness to the new levels or remain in the fourth dimensional frequencies. Those who choose to remain, will not be able to see you in your new creation any more than many of you cannot presently see the Masters that speak to you through these pages. You are fully aware that we exist but many of you cannot see us for the veil of dimensional frequency hides us from your present view. Just as we can see you, why do you suppose you can still see the fourth dimensional drama playing out in your world even though many of you feel a strong sense of being disconnected from it? Your ego still perceives through duality, and what you are witnessing is not a split in the worlds, but rather your own expansion into higher resonating dimensions. Perhaps this sheds new Light on your questions of the illusion of your world splitting in two rather than the all inclusive multidimensional reality of "worlds within worlds." If you choose to perceive your world splitting in two, know that you are seeing through the ego's eyes that see double. Shift your perceptions to the eye that is singular and see the "both/and" of both your new creation overlaid upon the potential of the fourth dimensional world that your

91

consciousness is expanding beyond. Those of you that have already shifted your consciousness into the energies of the fifth, sixth and seventh dimensions, can still see the fourth dimensional world. Perhaps you have not yet considered that when you harness these highly refined frequencies of energy it is causing those still locked within the fourth dimension to kick up fear in greater resistance, as well as your own ego's kicking up the fear. It takes the workers in the Light to set the tone of ascension on your plane attuned to the Masters on the higher resonating frequencies. This in turn agitates those around you that through either denial or their own ignorance are unable to raise their resonance. Did you think that all of your concentrated effort to meditate in groups around the world is not having its impact? How little you understand of your own power. You are and have been holding the higher resonance and this is how the earth is ascending into the higher frequencies. We are always and a day here to assist you in holding our resonance higher still to instigate you to always reach for more. Another reminder is offered that expansion is always inclusive and that you are far more powerful than you allow yourself to embrace. With this preface said, we offer you more guidelines and encourage you to now set about aligning in Group Soul effort in the furtherance of your work.

Understand that the workers in the Light on your earth plane are also an integral part of the Ascended Host. Our role is to hold our resonance so that you may lift yours to where we are. Your role is to lift your resonance in degrees and stages and then hold the resonance at each level so that your world of greater humanity can lift their resonance to where you are.

Great shifts in consciousness bring about great changes in the world. Great shifts in consciousness are the precursor of building the Cities of Light. There can be no success in this endeavor without groups of Light beings awakened in harmonic unison. In all things considered as your past, within the cycling revolutions of historical times, the individual personality was the focus of spiritual endeavor, yet great rifts in consciousness pervaded. In all things forward, communion of the Group Soul must be activated to carry out the next phase of Divine Plan. It is imperative that the next phase of the awakening of Group Soul effort be executed. Great shifts make way to mend the great rifts.

Work to clear the inner path is work that clears the path of those that follow. This is the work of the preliminary stages to prepare the individual for Group Soul effort. Healing work of this nature has been ongoing and successful. Continued efforts along this course enhance the Great Work on all levels. Now understand this that a World Server is only as worthy to serve humanity as his/her own sense of self-worth. Any worker that has a low sense of self-worth hinders humanity from progressing on its path for it is the worker in the Light that must show by example the worth and value of all human life. A World Server is only as forgiving of humanity as his/her own ability to forgive self. Any worker unwilling to forgive his/her own self-perceived transgressions hinders humanity from moving more fully into the state of grace. A World Server is only as integral to the unifying of the whole as his/her ability to act with spiritual integrity. Any worker unable to maintain his/her spiritual integrity hinders humanity from rising above degradation and denigration. All healing occurs with the understanding that the power is within each and every one of you. We are aware that this most important truth has become a spiritual catch phrase in your world. Heed this message for to diminish the truth of this statement is to render you powerless to incite healing on any level. What is healing but attunement of the conscious mind to the Higher Consciousness? There is a fine balance of knowing when the spiritual human being must shift the focus from the personal path in readiness for Group Soul effort for many get waylaid in the repetition of their individual lessons and healing adjustments. There comes a point when the spiritual human being must arrive at full self-acceptance and self-love. The time has long been nigh to say masterfully of the healing, *"It is accomplished."*

It is the task of the World Servers to set the example through word and deed. Behavior is the mirror of evolution. Look into the mirror of your own behavior. Avoid casting aversion on others. Whereas individual behavior is indicative of the level of individual soul growth, likewise group behavior is reflective of the evolution of the Group Soul. Group efforts that are swayed by individual ego aspersion delay progress of both the individual as well as the entire group. Any individual worker in the Light that does not support the other workers in their efforts is not attuned to the Group Soul resonance. For such time being, it is best for them to continue with their individual progress until they are ready to unite their focus with the group. All spiritual work endeavored on the individual level also adds its energy in uplifting the global community.

There are two avenues of powerful impact upon your dimensions. One is the state of being we speak of as the qualities of the Soul essence. As these essences are embodied, the higher vibrations shift the resonance of the individual body, as well as the global body of humanity. Being in the world in this manner shifts the energy in the immediate sector of influence, as well as adds to the overall uplifting of the collective of humanity.

Second of the avenues of impact is the conscious intent by the workers in the Light of harnessing energy through single-pointed focus to infuse the dimensions with the Light of intelligent awareness of high ideal. The first method comes about through the purification and refinement of the thoughts and emotions to that of the higher essences referenced as the temple of the Soul. The second method is brought about through meditative focus of intent with great discipline to not waver the thoughts to the denser fear based resonance but to hold the single-pointed focus of the higher ideal. In this meditative process the intent is fixed on the ideal vision and impressed upon the dimensional frequencies to re-pattern the old imagery made manifest in your world. Although either of the two paths of impact has power in its own effect, mastery includes the unification of both of these methods and avenues in the creation and manifestation process. Impact of the essence of the Soul combined with the infusion of the Light of Spirit is the goal towards balance that produces harmony.

Harnessing Cosmic energy in the single-pointed focus of Group Soul effort brings about exponential results. If there is struggle involved, it is a sign of the ego's intrusion into the effort. When all workers in the Group Soul are aligned in harmonious rapport, the way is made clear. Mountains, whether they are literal or intangible obstacles, cannot resist the command to move from the combined efforts of the Group Soul. Be ever mindful that the efforts of Group Soul are only orchestrated through the focus of the Master Creator God being to be made manifest on your plane. Through your Higher Consciousness, you are the conductors of your own harmonic resonance.

The center of the cross is the balancing of the single-pointed focus extended in all of the fourth dimensional directions. At the center of the star is the essence that you are and the balancing of the single-pointed focus extended in all of the fifth dimensional directions. The seat of power is always at the center of converging points. When all points converge into the center, the center must expand outward. This is the Law of the Ages. The One is the All, the many named and the yet to be named. How much power is concentrated and harnessed by the many on the one-pointed focus? This is the power needed to generate the ascension of the collective aligned with the Gaia mind, otherwise it is an individual ascension or ascension in small groupings. The center point is equal to all distant points. The center point is the great equalizer. It is the balancing of power. Power to any one side or the other of the center point is power gone astray. The center point balance is such a delicate thing, that only one-pointed focus will maintain such a balance. Concentrated effort on such a focus is well worth the energy saved from being constantly expended to regain balance. Such wasted energy is not aligned with the Law of Elegance. Consciousness that swings to and fro like a pendulum causes a frantic dispersal of powerful energy.

The Group Soul is of unified purpose. Its highest purpose is first and foremost focussed on unification. The fruits of your labor will not be evident to the greater portion of humanity for years to come. However, you will taste of the fruits of your labor in the immediacy of your alignment with Higher Purpose. Your rewards will be reaped from the Great Work itself. If you are seeking to serve ego, you are not aligned with Higher Purpose. If you are looking for rewards that serve the ego, you are not aligned with Higher Purpose. The ego will seek recognition, fame, glory and personal attention. The ego will seek attention in any and all manner and will likewise attempt to distract others from the path of Group Soul effort. In its clever disguise the ego will often deceive you into believing that you are aligned with best intentions when indeed it is its main goal to distract you from your Higher Purpose. The ego is self-serving rather than of service to humanity. The rewards of the ego are short lived. Rewards of Higher Purpose are infinite and eternal. That is not to say that suffering or lack is involved in being of World Service. These are mindsets that have long been outdated and need to be purged from the collective consciousness. In all Group Soul endeavor, any attachment to outcome that is not aligned with Divine Plan is ego based and will create friction among the ranks of the workers. Each worker must release all attachment to outcomes that serve the personal gain of the individual ego. Moments of self-doubt are conquered through pure faith and Group Soul effort. This is not to say that the individual Soul will not continue to grow and expand their consciousness within the Group Soul effort. As is the Law of Elegance, when the One is served the All is served, and when the All is served the One is served.

Each individual Soul carries certain keys, and it is within the template of the design that you connect with your Group Soul to bring forth the energy of the combination of these keys. Although any individual can access directly through to the Source energy for the purposes of individual evolution and personal creation process, there is a certain harmonic that is pre-encoded on the Soul imprint to awaken and connect with others in the Group Soul effort. This is a built in safeguard to ensure that no one person could attain unlimited power to abuse or misuse towards individual ends at the level of earth plane creation. Predominant within Divine Plan of the Group Soul effort is the basis of unification. We emphasize the importance of unification due to this built in safeguard to ensure that the individual ego is subverted in order for the collective Group Soul consciousness to unify in harmony. There is no harmony without unification. The Law of Elegance is employed in that the very basis of unification depends on Group Soul effort. Unifying the individuals into Group Soul also opens up the way for the use of harmonics. Herein we offer you a greater understanding of the truth that harmony is key to the new creation. This statement of truth is replete with multidimensional layers of meaning. Keys and codes accessed will apply to the level of the work and are sourced in the fire codes and sacred geometries many of which are beyond your present comprehension. Allow them to be revealed to you in your inner vision. Seek the understanding of direct access to the keys and codes. Revelation is inherent in the energy pre-encoded in the keys. We clarify this statement further by saying that the pre-encoded keys will cause revelation of their purpose when they are accessed. Revelations will trigger further awakenings to the multidimensional realms. Each key and code is a threshold of consciousness to be attained on both the individual and group level.

Each individuated awakened Soul within the Group Soul resonates at a particular harmonic, which is in accord with the other members of the group. Each individuated awakened Soul will recognize their Group Soul by their tone in the harmonic. Colors of the individuals compliment one another. Their combined tones create a symphony that will drown out all the cacophony of discordant vibration. The combined colors of the individuals within the Group Soul create a new level of spiritual essence, which will be emanated as the group whole. Once more, we ask you tarry not on the issue of color. Do not remain stagnant in simply one color frequency. There are certain colors that any individual will resonate with more at certain times. Throughout any life expression there will be certain colors that are more prominent as the life Ray and Flame bandwidth of frequency vibration inherent in the Higher Purpose. However, the radiance of the colors like all things will shift and change within the group similar to the shifting colors of the individual aura. It is as if you are all players in a symphony orchestra and some of you may be able to play more than one instrument. For certain pieces of creation of the symphony, you may put down one instrument and rather play another to bring forth the particular sound needed. This is how it is meant to be. To ask any individual to remain locked within an experience of a singular color emanation would prevent the individual, as well as the Group Soul effort, to progress. Be flexible, be forbearing, be free, be flowing, and be the movement that is consciousness that breathes itself into creation and sits at the threshold of reflection through expansion and contraction. Herein again is the paradox we must urge you to embrace. Group Soul must remain in single-pointed focus to bring about the desired results into manifestation, yet we say that to be flexible is also of great import. Let us clarify to say that single-pointed focus through unification of the ideal must be held with out a single iota of wavering thought process. Still we say that within that single-pointed focus toward the end goal of manifestation there needs to be flexibility in the way of Divine Love. Love is flexible and forbearing, yet discipline of the mental thoughts aligned with Higher Purpose in unified effort must be adhered to.

Alignment of the telepathic and empathic energies between spiritual human beings is the fusion of Group Soul. For just an instant imagine the power of the fusion principle of your physics that generates your sun's energy and then understand the same principle applied to the fusion of the Group Soul effort.

Now we must impress upon you an even greater understanding of how the creation principle works its miracles within the Group Soul effort. While each individual Soul makes its imprint on the Group Soul, the combination of all Souls in the Group in essence creates a new entity. We urge you to see the beauty and magnificence of the creation principle inherent in all endeavors. This is why we tell you to allow for Groups of Souls to come together in unified purpose and to also allow for the changes that all evolution brings about. With each new creation of Group Souls, a new entity is born as the group. When any group disperses this is again a transition no different than a death of anything or anyone. It is all simply change. Consciousness shifts its focus and change occurs. To hold the one-pointed focus for any purpose will always have an outcome in the fields of creation. Expand your consciousness to comprehend that the process to create as an individual from an idea and bring forth this idea into your world is no different than to create from the Group Soul effort to bring an idealized vision forth into your world. Raising the level of vibration of an idea to that of the envisioned ideal is a vital part of the ascension process. However, Group Soul effort does take a considerable amount of evolved beings utilizing a considerable amount more of focused consciousness to activate more potent energy. Group Soul effort can accomplish far more in the scheme of Divine Plan on your plane than any single individual at this point in your conscious evolution.

To add further to your understanding, uniting individuated Souls into the Group Soul creates yet another level of the merkaba, which is the Group Soul merkaba. Each unique tone of the individuated Soul within the Group Soul activates one of the points on the Group Soul merkaba in its focus, which in turn creates the three-fold reflection process on the facets. Now you see that you can disperse certain energies in the Group Soul merkaba to reunite in different coordinates with other members to create yet another new and unique Group Soul merkaba to put forth in your efforts. This once again we bring to your attention is the beauty and magnificent splendor of the infinitude of creation.

Every step along the way in learning to consciously create is a process towards becoming a Master Creator God being. The Ascended Host creates through both individual and Group Soul effort, and no one individual entity takes credit for the universal creation. Your universe and galactic systems of planets are created through the efforts of what we refer to as the Master Creator God beings and the Ascended Host through varying frequencies of consciousness. This effort exudes from the threshold of Source throughout the entire reaches of this local universe, as well as numerous adjacent universes and worlds within worlds. Powerful energies of creation are accessed from this threshold and extended into the multidimensional realms of resonant vibration. Other universal plans are under the guidance of other entities, as well as many of the members of the Ascended Host involved in your universe. Perhaps this gives you a greater clue as to how many multidimensional realms our focus is concentrated on.

New foundations cannot be built on true harmony or peace without the blending of the harmonics of the Group Soul. Therefore, those that are still focussed in the individual personality stage will not find their group of workers until they awaken to the Group Soul level. As long as the individual entertains the distractions of the ego, he/she will not attract in other members of the Group Soul. This is not to say that the uniqueness of any individual will be swallowed up in the ocean of greater being for that is never the case in the evolutionary design, but each unique Soul adds a special ingredient to make a more enhanced creation.

With the blending of the harmonics of the Group Soul, the resonance of the group is raised. Combined efforts of the Group Soul raise the resonance in alignment with the ascension of the Gaia planetary consciousness. Beyond your plane, the layers of harmonics within each Group Soul resonate to members of the Ascended Host in the higher resonating multi-dimensional levels of consciousness. In this way, the combined efforts to align and elevate the frequencies of resonance create a new level of resonance on the planet. Those not attuned to this new frequency may react with agitation, as they are not accustomed to the higher frequency vibrations. It can cause irritation to the emotional body to erupt more frequently amongst the uninitiated individual, as well as the workers in the Light. Great caution should be taken to not indulge in ego confrontation caused by the agitation. All workers in the Light are to hold the resonance high, for any lowering of the resonance puts the World Server out of tune with the greater rhythm of the ascension process. Allowing the ego to react with agitation adds more friction and agitation to the ongoing friction of those that resist the escalating energies. Set the tone by being the tone.

Color is key to understanding the tone to be set. Awareness of color and tone is an aid to the worker on the path, for these are the tools of the harmonics that will be used to direct and focus energy. Those that remain within the primary color palette of creation, the basic reds, blues and yellows, are those in the initial stages of their Soul path. Group Soul colors are distinguished by the Rays and Flames, and tasks are marked accordingly by the essence of the radiant tonal frequency. Information can be gleaned as to the spiritual essence of the harmonic tone by the word descriptive of Gold/Silver, iridescence, and pearlescence to name a few. It is not possible to indicate all the varying levels of the color/tonal frequencies for it is beyond the constraints of your language. Stretch your minds around the truth that as infinite as number is so is the infinity of color and tonal variation. A reminder is once again offered that you are the portal to the multidimensional frequencies, and this text is intended as a guide to awakening your consciousness to experience more of your multidimensional reality. Some of the color/tonal frequencies are not translatable in your current understanding, and others are yet to be created by the future combination of Group Soul energies. How do you describe in your language the iridescent, coppery sparkle infused with pearlescent overtones? The example in this previous sentence can only allude to the reality at best. You cannot really grasp the energy of the higher vibratory tones or the Language of Light in the limitations of your linear language. Experience the colors by being the colors. Open to the frequencies of the fire codes and let them infuse your consciousness with the solar fire of pure intent. Understanding the color/tonal frequencies will come with the ease of awakening to these levels of conscious awareness. Working with the color/tonal energies is a practice set forth by utilizing the inner plane sensory apparatus. The inner senses will reflect these higher resonating color/tonal energies, and the tasks of the Group Soul will be focussed along the same color/tonal energy bands. It is not completely necessary to fully understand the colors/tones if one is taking up directive and action intuitively aligned with the energies. However, any measure of your understanding aids the individual and Group Soul in the work at hand. A certain level of understanding is necessary to the work, but do not be overly concerned with a total comprehension before moving forward. Waiting for total comprehension is another fear-based ego excuse, for the full breadth of knowledge will never be attained. All current levels of manifestation of these tones on your earth plane are but a dim reflection of the pure and refined essence of the true harmonic level. Even those workers in the Light that currently radiate the higher essences of the radiant colors will attain new levels of emanating these energies. Always seek the highest level of the tonal radiant. If it is beyond your current awareness level, stretch and reach and ask for guidance. Allow the color/tonal frequency to teach you. Experiment, explore, and experience the color/tonal frequency. Merge into the experience and re-emerge upon higher levels of existence. These will constitute the first layers of your experience for harmonic dimensions exist far beyond these preliminary levels of the radiation of spiritual essence. Cities of Light will initially be constructed from these initiatory levels of manifestation along the energy bands of the Rays and Flames. Practice towards crystallizing the Group Soul thought forms will need to be applied repeatedly with each level of success achieved.

Do not dismay if some enter the Group Soul effort and then shift their focus otherwise. This may occur for a number of reasons. Either the individual is not yet prepared to commit to the Group Soul to the intensity that is required, or the individual may add their energy to the Group Soul for a required outcome and will depart the group effort when the outcome is achieved. We caution you to not judge any individual's participation in any effort. Look only to your own level of commitment in the areas you are called to fulfill. Discernment of your own path in combination with the individual discernment of each of your fellow workers will bring all together in harmonious unison toward Group Soul unification of Higher Purpose. Any assessment of another's level of participation is yet another distraction of the ego. How many are in a group? Whenever two or more are gathered the intent of focus is amplified through the law of number. Two within a group focus is multiplied exponentially to the power of two, which results in a focus of four. Three within a group focus is multiplied exponentially to the power of three, which results in a focus of nine, while four within a group focus is multiplied exponentially to the power of four resulting in a focus of sixteen, etc.

Within the overall design, there are many fail-safe systems within the greater Divine Plan to insure that all roads lead home. If any worker in the Light falls by the wayside and wearies of their focus, there are always those in waiting prepared to take up the task when they are called.

Universal plans of evolution pervade the greater Cosmos. Each plan is instigated accordingly from the assessment at the highest levels directly from Source. Each universal plan is unique to its own universal scheme. Master Creators are the designers accessing the powerful energies at the Source of the Almighty One. Beyond these levels of creation from the design of the Master Creator God beings, is the incomprehensible One. It is naught for you to try to attain the full implications of this level that is far beyond your grasp at this point in your evolutionary awakening. Expanding your consciousness into the infinite and incomprehensible One is always the goal of Divine Plan, but the intensities of the frequencies at Source must be approached in steps and stages of your conscious awakening. Do not belittle yourself at your stage in comparisons to the infinite nature of the Source of your existence, for you are far more powerful than you will allow yourself to be. Simply be aware of the necessity to continue to expand your awareness in ever increasing degrees of freedom of expression and grasp of the complexities of your true nature. Just to tap into a mere iota of energy at Source is a power enough for a Master Creator God being to sustain the creation of many universes. Do you not see the magnitude of power that is available to you that is already within your grasp? In accord with unification, the Master Creators and the Ascended Host work in complete unification towards all goals to bring about the idealized visions of the Elohim. Do you not see the magnitude of power that will be focused when the workers in the Light on your plane are unified in Group Soul efforts with the Ascended Host? Be alert in your vigilance to not allow the understanding of the potency of this unified power to slip past your conscious grasp lest you miss the wonderment of this opportunity to bring forth the magnificent harmony of the Golden Age made manifest.

Divine Plan is dependent upon you more so than you being dependent on Divine Plan. Many are those that stray, but few are those that adhere to these principles. Strength of commitment is the fortitude that shall bring forth the unification of Group Soul effort. Group effort of cooperation is inherent within all multidimensional levels of consciousness, for cooperation is a feminine aspect of the Love that is Divine. We, the Ascended Host, are aligned in Group effort along with the workers in Light on your plane. You have the support of the entire Ascended Host for it is our commitment to be with you ever and a day in accord with our oath to serve you. All workers in the Light that serve your world likewise serve the Ascended Host on behalf of the One. You arrive again at the crossroads of paradox for we will say it is a two-way effort, but in reality there is no separation for your work is our work and our work is your work.

Merging into the work of Group Soul is not a loss of individual consciousness but rather a unification of effort towards a particular goal. The goals of the Group Soul effort are always and ever in accord with the higher frequencies of Divine Plan. However, the individual is always attaining more freedom within this work towards the goal of becoming the Master Creator God being that is each and everyone's birthright. Once again, we warn you that it is only the ego's voice that places the limitations upon your efforts. Group Soul effort is an aspect of working within the Divine Plan of evolution for your universal frequency code. All frequency codes are attuned to Divine Plan, and your efforts to awaken and activate your codes work in conjunction with the accelerated frequencies. With each step you take, expansion is ever upon you into the eternal and incomprehensible reality of infinity.

Unification at your current level of attention is attraction of like mind and attraction of like cause put into effect. This is the goal of Group Soul effort. When the Group Soul awakens to the unified idealized vision and implements it through Group Soul effort, the vision will be imparted to your world. The vision will initially be overlaid as an etheric template to impress upon the etheric dimensional frequencies as the blueprint to be brought to fruition. As the vision materializes and the new creation is birthed, humanity will stand in awe and wonder why had it not always been this way. There will be those that will know that truth has always been this way but its arrival had been awaiting the preparation. Those in the know will be the awakened Group Soul. As the architects of Light radiate the new creation from out of the center of the Heart of Hearts, it shall create the space for each and every Heart to awaken in the harmony and beauty made manifest.

FIVE

CITIES OF LIGHT

There shall come to pass the glory of heaven
upon the countenance of the earth,
and it will be born in the Cities of Light.

Light is Divine Love awakened from its dark slumber. What other is the dark slumber but Divine Love that is not fully realized and freely expressed? What then is a City of Light but the communal manifestation of Divine Love?

We speak both metaphorically and literally for the Light will be made manifest in the new creation. Where there was no Light before, stars will shine. Where there was only darkness hiding in its own shadowy spaces, the daughters and sons of suns will shine. The awakened spiritual human being will glow with the brilliant Golden White Light of Divine Love. Whenever two or more are gathered, the collective of awakened spiritual human beings will create the glow of a City of Light. All will be illuminated from within and such will be the luminosity of the Cities of Light and those that walk the Golden pathways of the stars.

Balancing of the powerful energies of creation with a purified consciousness through the Heart/mind is the high wire feat to be accomplished. Maintaining this balance is fraught with the precarious challenges of any finely honed craft. Creation is an art form in every sense of the word. Layers of meaning are to be found in this singular statement. Each word in this statement alone is filled with multidimensional layers of meaning. Separate each individual word and delve into the layers of meaning. The words, "creation," "art," "form," and "sense" hold keys to the mystery of evolution all within their combined letters. Within the phrase *"The Word"* you have heard us speak often of the potent forces of creation that are unleashed upon declaration of "The Word." As "The Word" issues forth, "creation" is "art" in "form," and the "senses" reflect upon the "creation." This is only one of many ways to reread the meaning. Now upon reading these further clues to the depth of multidimensional layers of meaning in The Word, we make the statement again as an exercise for you to awaken to the multidimensional frequencies within a single sentence. *"Creation is an art form in every sense of the word."* Can you now see the power of revelation within "The Word?" Can you now catch a glimpse of the layers of mystery in creation yet to be uncovered? Can you begin to stretch your consciousness to fathom the variety of possibilities of rearranging the letters, which are vibrations that are infinite in frequency of number?

Your words spring forth from your thought process but your thought process of ideas is not always aligned with the highest vibration of the mental plane of ideals. Each plane has varying levels and degrees of vibration also. The physical body can vibrate at the densest level of ill health and suffering aligned with an emotional body vibrating at the same level of ill feelings, aligned with a mental body vibrating at the same level of ill thoughts of suffering and limitations of pain. In this same way, the physical body is also able to vibrate at its highest level of wellbeing, aligned with an emotional body vibrating at the level of joy, aligned with a mental body vibrating at the level of an ideal of Divine Love. Within these ranges are many degrees in between of synthesizing the four body system. Expand your consciousness into the twelve-chakra body system and there are also ranges of vibration within each level of that system. Perhaps you now understand more fully why we continuously remind you to monitor your thoughts and to choose your words carefully.

Freedom from limitation is ever a goal upon the path, for it is not in the infinite and eternal nature of consciousness to place boundaries upon its expression. Elegance is the most direct path for it embodies the law of maximum return for minimum energy expended. These laws are inherent in the Cosmic energies emanating from Divine Source, and any particle of energy in the fallen continuum not aligned with these laws will be subject to perfected correction in alignment with Divine Source. All is on its course to return to Source fully perfected to then go forth again and create anew. Let us guide you towards a new understanding of the term "perfection." Once more, we issue warning to not give this ideal of perfection over to the ego's level of interpretation for it will fill your thoughts with limiting images of your imperfections through the dual eyes of comparison. Perfection is not a static state of existence or creation. Perfection is the ideal of harmonic resonance. Like any symphony perfectly and beautifully orchestrated, the ideals of harmonic resonance pulse a rhythm. A symphony is not static as it ripples its tones across space to bathe each listener in its harmonious resonance. Likewise, each listener responds in their own unique vibration of harmony. Attunement to this cosmic rhythm of harmonic resonance will allow the manifestation of many more beautiful creations to emanate on your plane spontaneously within each present moment. Ideals are imprinted upon the etheric fields of creation, and it is to this goal that Divine Plan unfolds within all levels of creation. Let it be known that each level of enhancement within the creation is only a precedent to the next level of perfection achieved. If you could imagine a holographic image of many layers of overlaying design, you could begin to grasp the understanding of the blueprints of Divine Plan and the template of perfection to be achieved. This is but one view of the template of the Adam Kadmon design that is overlaid upon the physical human animal, the human being, and the spiritual human being and further still into the Master Creator God being. Achievement of this perfected design into the fields of creation shall perform feats far grander than your fathers before you. We do not refer to your physical fathers but to that of your spiritual fathers. The new creation is a model of perfection within the ever-expanding evolution of Divine Plan. This perfection is the tone of pure harmony of the sum of all of its parts. Each stage of perfecting the creation is vital to the outcome. Our emphasis on self-acceptance through self-love at each stage of creation prepares the way for the next level of expansion of consciousness into attaining more potential of the ideals of Divine Love.

Multidimensional layers of creation are the avenues of extension of consciousness. Through the power of creation at Divine Source, consciousness extends itself into the multidimensional frequencies of space. Therefore, when we suggest you extend yourself to your world in expression of the refined energies of spiritual essence, we wish to impress upon you the Divine principle at play in every action. As your consciousness attunes to the state of grace, you will extend yourself more graciously and move more gracefully through your world. As your consciousness attunes to the state of joy, you will extend joy to those around you. Joy is contagious and will instigate others to lift their Spirits to dance on air. As your consciousness attunes to the state of integrity, you will extend the awareness of how integral each part of humanity and consciousness is to the sum of the whole. Can you now see the meaning of honoring each other as you must honor your Self for each and everyone is integral to the equation. Each and everyone must hold themselves in the highest integrity and extend it towards each other.

Purity of vision is in the eye of the beholder. Allow the higher visions to entice you into their realm and behold the majesty of splendor. Become the enlivened template of the new creation. Pattern all manifestation on the highest of spiritual essence and ethics.

As we spoke of the living libraries of the Language of Light, let us enhance your understanding further upon this. The Cities of Light will have points of connection in the earth grid matrix. These grids are being activated and anchored in place by many workers of the Light co-creating the etheric template of the new creation in accord with the Ascended Host. Anchoring the Light takes a conscious duty to fulfill the chosen role working with the Ascended Host. Workers in the Light aligned with their purpose of grid activation are attuned to the tasks at hand and have carried on faithfully. After anchoring the Light in strategic places on the earth grid, the Light will be activated along the meridians through the efforts of both the Ascended Host and workers in the Light through Group Soul effort. Earth matrix meridians align with the meridians in the human body and also align with the stars. To simplify the understanding of the esoteric nature of this is simply to say that the points of Light that are stars are no different than the points of Light in the meridians of the human body and the earth body of Gaia consciousness. Activation is another term for alignment. However, it is a bit more complicated in terms of the application of the higher scientific achievement. Alignment and attunement of these points in the matrix is accomplished on many levels. Alignment through the conscious efforts of the workers in the Light with the conscious efforts of the Ascended Host and grid Masters activates the Light on the meridian points. The Light is synchronized in this manner. Light is intelligent self-awareness. It takes an evolved and intelligent self-aware worker in the Light to understand where the meridian points of the earth grid are and how to activate the attunements. There are those that specialize in this work, but you must understand also that each and every worker that activates the Light of conscious awareness within the individual self, as well as Group Soul effort, is working in alignment of these principles. We repeat that Light is intelligent self-awareness. Each cell in the human body is a sun in the making. As the human cells awaken through evolutionary enlightenment to becoming the spiritual human being, the DNA is activated and more Light emanates from within the cellular structure. As Gaia consciousness awakens to its own higher self of the planetary logos, Sanat Kumara, so too the body of the earth contains more Light in its sphere of consciousness influence. These alignments open more channels for the Ascended Host to communicate telepathically to the workers on the earth plane. Many meridian points have begun to be activated. As the meridians of the body of Gaia consciousness align with the meridians of the body of the human consciousness in attunement with the template of the stars, this activates the synapses of the galactic brain. Be mindful that your sun is a star also. Although many are unaware of the etheric network of the galactic body, we assure you that it exists in the similar manner that your nervous system is wired throughout your physical body. Through the temporal lobes of the galactic brain the codes and frequencies of the new creation are stored and then actively delivered along these points. The temporal lobes of the galactic brain feed the data of awakening the codes of the higher dimensional frequencies through the temporal lobes in the human brain. Perhaps you can see that when the meridians of the body of the spiritual human being are aligned with both the meridians of the Gaia consciousness and the template of the stars, the spiritual human being becomes the bridge of Light between the two. Not only is the spiritual human being a bridge, you are also a portal to other dimensional frequencies awakening the living libraries of the Language of Light. You have a very delicate job and hefty responsibility to maintain the equilibrium of the balance. Can you now see why we honor you in the importance of your role in Divine Plan?

When the grids are completely aligned with the matrices of Light, the meridians will be activated connecting the other small communal pockets of Light within the grid. Although there is a vast difference between what we perceive to be archaic forms of technical communication on your plane, telepathic rapport through these connected channels of Light can be likened to the limited versions of information transference via telephone wires, satellites and computers. Whereas the signal in your world once had to travel through the wire or reflect its beam off of a satellite dish, the brilliant white Light of intelligent conscious awareness through the activated meridians travels along the new matrix grid almost instantaneously. There will still be a lag in the transference of this information through the greater system. Even though the resonant frequency is rising above the old levels, the slight lapse will exist in the transmission of information for nothing occurs as instantaneous as being completely in the center of Source. Throughout all of the manifestation of creation, there is a rhythmic pulsation of the frequencies. Similar to the signals of the human brain traveling through the nervous system of the body, communication is transferred through the body of Gaia consciousness and the awakened spiritual human body and the star essence all merging the triad into one. In multidimensional terms of alignment, this awakens the three bodies into the one galactic body.

Now we will correlate this further to the four-body system comprised of the physical, emotional, mental and spiritual bodies. As consciousness expands, the spiritual body includes the realm of the mental, the emotional and the physical bodies. This is one aspect of the trinity of the three into one. Another aspect of the trinity of creation is that the Galactic body includes the star essence, the awakened spiritual human being, and the body of earth. These two examples of the significance of three in the creation principle comprises the formula of the trinity of creation back into the One. Once again we remind you that the trinity of creation is but one aspect of the basic formulas that permeate the multidimensional realms and also to reiterate that number is infinite, and, therefore, the numeric formulas become more complex as consciousness expands into infinity.

Communication between the Cities of Light and the various Group Souls will be the first to awaken to this level of telepathic rapport. Greater humanity will follow at a slower pace. Compare to the effects of a new technology in your world. When the telephone was invented and put into place, not everyone was connected by the telephone service. Little by little each neighborhood got wired to speak to the next neighborhood and so on around the globe. As the meridians on the earth grid matrix are activated, not everyone will be connected consciously via their

Higher Consciousness to utilize this telepathic system. Those who are already attuned are already tuned in. Each will connect when their time is nigh upon them. Until one is ready to focus on unification, he/she will remain unconnected to the matrix of Light. As long as the ego is self-serving, it will not be able to connect to the Light matrix. There is a higher explanation to the reason for this. Until one is ready to stand within the center of integrity and compassion, one is not allowed to have full access to the telepathic grid to use for the ego's purpose of manipulation and control. Until one has conquered the ego's negative tendencies, there will be very limited access to the higher resonating frequencies of telepathy. It is a safeguard within the system of Divine Plan that no entity can access the powerful energies at Source to use in a destructive manner in the lower fallen continuum. Therefore, although each individual and group in the lower resonating planes has the ability to destroy portions of creation through the ignorance of fear from the unconscious or the ego arrogance of abusing power, their abilities are limited to a partial plane aspect at the level of their consciousness existence. This safeguard is accomplished through the community of Divine Love and the greater good for all. Love will always and ever be potently more powerful than the destructive forces of the limited ego. As an example, if you were to multiply the magnitude of an atomic bomb in your reality by the largest number you could conceive of, you would not even begin to be close to the magnitude of the powerful energy at the Source. There is no finite number to equate to the infinity of the power at Source. Humanity currently exists in the finite dimensions of the fourth and a small portion of awakened humanity consciously exists in the fifth dimensions and greater. How do you suppose humankind could possibly create something that would have any destructive effect on the Source, which is infinitely omnipotent, omnipresent and omniscient?

Likewise, no one can gain access to the telepathic grid if one is aligned with negative intent to use the grid for malicious purpose. Mind control is only a detriment to the lower resonating levels of fear-based constituencies. This is not something to be concerned with when you are aligned with the resonance of Divine Love for Divine protection is inherent in the nature of Divine Love. How could it be otherwise? Would Divine Love leave you to the whims of some imaginary power outside itself? How could it when Divine Love is all-inclusive? Fear is a by-product of the limitations of ego. Fear does not and cannot exist within Divine Love. We speak of this repeatedly until you release the last remnants of your fear. Your fear is but the veil of illusion that you allow your ego to create which blinds you to these truths.

When we address each worker in the Light and remind you of how powerful you are, we address you as the ones that have learned about the abuse of power in your dimensions. You are the ones ready for graduation. Those that are still learning about the positive use of power versus the abuse of power will remain in their classrooms of learning before they are able to elevate to more powerful levels of creation. In this way, you can perceive that you are not better than those that are still learning but that your consciousness has over long periods of trial and error evolved to certain expanded levels beyond the need to serve the negative ego's destructive ends. Many of you have learned the lessons of abusing power by having misused power in certain life expressions and reaping the negative consequences. Therefore, isn't it those of you who should hold the most compassion for the error of the ways you see others presently following? Empathy is born through the experience of similarity. We would hasten to add that your individual reactions to perceiving the misuses by others on your plane is your own empathy to understand the great negative impact such abuse brings about. It would serve you best to subdue your over-reactions and instead courageously pick up your scepter of power to bring forth more Light through the compassion of Divine Love.

While the construction of the initial Cities of Light are being undertaken, the rest of humanity will continue on its course through the lower dimensional frequencies of fear. Do not mistake the understanding of our reference to construction to be similar to the term used in your present day world. Construction will not initially take place with hammers and tools, although there will be a few incidents of the beginnings towards this end. All references to the construction of Cities of Light in the initial stages are accomplished through the awakening matrix of Light along the earth grid and in pockets of groups beginning to unify in their efforts. Building the foundation of the spiritual ethics within the individual Soul and Group Soul elicits the connection of the community of Light through the etheric web. When this connection is concentrated to the degree necessary for proper focus, then the externalization through manifestation of the building of the communities will be forthcoming.

The areas throughout the earth of building the communities of Light will be far and few in the first wave of this phase of unfolding plan. Gradually, as the Light increases in the consciousness of humanity, there will be more areas of Light made manifest through building communities of Light worldwide. No two communities will be the same, but each will be designed upon the foundations of the highest spiritual ethics. Creativity inherent within the creation principle does not limit itself to the mass production or cloning of ideas and the present type of manifestation that greater humanity has become accustomed to. Mass production is not a component of the new creation.

All needs are fulfilled for each and every one through the Law of Abundance. There is no shortage to energy in the Cosmos, and therefore, there is no shortage to abundant manifestation. It is better to ask the aspiring student or the World Server if the abundance they seek is for empty ego gratification or if the wealth of beauty would rather be made manifest for all to enjoy. It might seem apparent that there are many things produced in your world that have no real value or worth in light of the essence of the Soul. Halls and warehouses of products to delight the passing fancy of instant gratification of the ego's search for fulfillment can very well be shifted into interactive gathering places of art and beauty to offer nurturing sustenance to the Soul. Unified participation of meaningful intent brings about the movement of the Spirit upon the deep waters of the Soul stirring up more movement of the energy of creation. Renewal is inherent in the new creation. Revitalization and self-perpetuating creative energy are your tools supplied by Source.

Concern over the linear timeline of accomplishment of the Great Work is an ego distraction. The Ascended Host does not concern itself with dates of completion. There is no place for such distraction at the level of the Ascended Host, whose task it is to hold the one-pointed focus of idealized vision throughout millennia. Overcome any notions that the One Source is on a set schedule. It is true that the Source energy of creation is pulsating a rhythm of creation into a multitude of universes, as well as it is also true that many Lords of Creation are utilizing the energy at Source and creating universes, galaxies, planets and species. Would you suppose that the One Source of Almighty power places limitations on the infinitude of manifested creation capable by its offspring? Do you not see the powerful beings you are when you understand that there is no such limit on your power to create other than the limits you place upon yourselves, as well as your ability to comprehend the ineffable complexities of creation? Only your conscious level of evolution is a hindrance to expanding your power into greater accomplishments, and your evolutionary plan is perfectly designed to awaken you towards these goals. Do you not recognize the wisdom then to cooperate with your evolutionary plan rather than resist it? Cooperation is imperative in the new creation of the Cities of Light. Energy of creation pulsates in rhythmic tones. One is either in tune with the rhythm or out of step. Do you not see the humor that the timepiece worn on the wrist is called "a watch" because the ego is always watching time fly by or drag on? We simply say the time is now. It is always now and always will be now. When you find you are out of step, pace yourself to the greater rhythmic pulse. Do this by slowing down and centering the consciousness within the center point of your existence to align with your Higher Consciousness. Being in tune is a form of cooperation. Resistance creates discordant frequencies that interfere with the pulsating rhythm. Intensifying energies you are sensing are indications of your sensitivity to the higher frequencies of resonance. Many of you are still trying to understand this higher frequency vibration through the fourth dimensional perception and attempting to understand its characteristics by your old paradigm standards of time measurement. It is not a matter of trying to measure this higher vibration, but rather it is a matter of *becoming* this new vibration. What we convey to you of utmost importance is to allow your physical, mental and emotional bodies to *become* the higher vibration rather than resist it.

In the same manner with which we tell you that the present moment is the only moment to be concerned with, we guide you to understand that within the power of the present moment is the only way to access the higher dimensional frequencies. When you are centered in the present moment at the threshold of the multidimensional energies, your consciousness will attune to exactly where in the rhythm of the cosmic pulse the evolution of Divine Plan is enacting on the earth plane and precisely your own individuated specificity within each moment. By being attuned to the greater cosmic rhythm of unfolding evolution, your consciousness will intuit how to harness the energies to be used in co-creating the new creation along with the Ascended Host.

The beauty of paradox is in its truth. Seemingly contradictory, it is only due to your limited perspective. Is there not the beauty of paradox in the statement, "It is accomplished," yet we tell you there are many tasks to be done? How do you reconcile paradox? Merge the duality into the one. Perceive through the singular eye. One must go about their tasks with the absolute faith in seeing the task as already accomplished. In like manner, we say there is no set schedule yet we urge you to not tarry and to make all efforts towards implementation of the next phase of Divine Plan. Such contradictions you behold are of your own lack of ability to grasp the sixth dimensional awareness level of paradox. We urge you to hasten your efforts and focus your one-pointed consciousness as a discipline of mastery. Otherwise, you will inevitably allow your ego to make petty excuses of procrastination. Any and all insistence on the part of the Ascended Host of the importance to accelerate your efforts on behalf of the Great Work is found in our role to keep you pointed towards your spiritual direction and away from the distractions of the ego. We address these issues of timelines and schedules for this is something that you are preoccupied with on your revolving cycles of fourth dimensional time rotations. Understand the pulsing rhythm of cosmic creation to be in the form of resonant waves of harmonic frequency. As the ascension of Gaia consciousness along with the ascension of human consciousness reaches higher dimensional frequencies, the waves of harmonic rhythms accelerate in frequency. With this acceleration of frequencies, the energies to manifest the new creation of the Golden Age are presently available. However, the rhythm of the waves of harmonics estimates the attainment of these goals worldwide to be what you would perceive from your vantage point as much further in the earth plane future times. From your perspective this explanation that there is only the present moment of now and waves of unfolding creation would appear to be wrapped in paradox within another paradox. This is indeed true that your consciousness must learn to balance these multidimensional perplexities, for when you are continuously focussed on the fourth dimensional version of your experiences, there are far many more levels of truths to encounter in the layered spheres of conscious awareness. Even within all of this explanation of resonant frequencies of conscious creation, we wish to simplify by bringing your attention once again to the Heart of the matter by simply stating the time is always now. The present moment is always the point of power, and it is from this point of power that all things stream forth from the One. Now to merge duality into the single-pointed focus of consciousness is the task at hand, and, by doing so, you will have the energy of Source available to serve you each moment in the palm of your hand.

A simple exercise for holding consciousness in the balance of paradox we offer is to hold the conscious thoughts on apparently dualistic opposites. You can begin by practicing holding the thoughts on both hot and cold simultaneously. When you find your thoughts shifting from hot to cold, merge them together. Observe the experience of your consciousness as you vacillate between one or the other until you have arrived at the merging of the dualities of "both/and." Practice embracing the truth in the statement, "It is both hot and cold, and there is no separation between them." This practice can be applied to all duality. Focus the mind on both turning left and turning right. Do this repeatedly until you realize that there is no direction at all. When you arrive at a place that you feel to be in a complete state of being without any sense of direction outside yourself, you will have tackled this exercise. When you feel to have attained sufficient adeptness, do not be overly concerned with perfecting this exercise and move your consciousness to another area of focus. It is merely a simple practice to stretch your consciousness into the fifth and sixth dimensional frequencies. We work with you in never-ending ways to expand your limited conscious mind into the infinity of the Higher Consciousness. In order for you to grasp the concept of the idealized vision of the Cities of Light, we must guide you to increase your understanding as well as hone your intuitive awareness. You must each and every one attain a certain level of comprehension before proceeding to work consciously on directing the energies of creation into the manifestation of the Cities of Light. Meditation on the dimensional seals offered earlier in this work is also another exercise in holding the consciousness on more levels than you are currently accustomed to.

The Cities of Light will be based on the foundation of unity. Unity is not confined to the definition of unifying with others of like purpose. Unity also involves unifying the dimensions all within the one-pointed focus of the conscious mind. These conscious and meditative exercises we offer are in preparation of Group Soul effort to reveal the harmony of unifying duality into oneness and merging the dimensions.

As you unify your energies to create the beginning foundations for the Cities of Light, you will be setting a new pattern in consciousness. Many of you are awaiting the hundredth monkey to awaken so that everyone will get on the bandwagon so to speak. Who is it that you think will be this hundredth person? How will they quantum leap their awareness into the escalated program of evolution if you are not the ones setting the pattern in consciousness for them to leap into? We jest with you playfully to entice you to step into your power, yet we are most serious in our endeavors to guide you to deeper understandings of your importance in being the initiators of the new creation. Those who are initiated are the initiators. How could it be otherwise?

We have imparted the truth that knowledge is power and that Light is self-aware intelligence. Likewise, energy is neutral, and consciousness places its intent upon the energies of creation. When the Light of intelligent self-awareness places its intent upon the energies of creation to manifest a City of Light, what then will be the outcome? We are aware of many on your plane waiting for instructions or wandering around in a lost maze, and we are aware of how many of you do not use the brilliant Light of your intelligent awareness to place your intent towards manifesting the Golden Age. Those who choose to be passive observers waiting for the judgment day or the day of reckoning or someone to rescue or save them will miss the opportunity of the millennia to participate in this most momentous occasion. You are the creators of the Golden Age, and it waits upon you to birth it into manifestation.

Here it is also with most serious intent to impress upon you to not give this understanding of your role in Divine Plan to your ego to feel superior to your family of humanity. The moment you do this is the moment you deplete your power to elicit such change towards unification.

It is a fine balancing act to claim your power and to remain humble. Humility is a requirement of this work. As humility is the path to the temple door, sacredness is the sanctity at its core.

Upon the foundations of the Temple of the Soul the pillars of Light shine in all their glory, and this we herald to be the forthcoming Cities of Light.

SIX

MODELS OF HARMONIC LIVING

*Through harmony shall the new creation
be uplifted on the wings of the dove.*

Harmonics converge and diverge, and pulsing waves of harmonics align in accord. What do we mean by this word harmonics? You understand music in your world to be in octaves, and each octave has a harmonic above and below in its frequency range. We reiterate once more to say that all is vibration. When consciousness vibrating at your level of resonance aligns with the higher frequencies of the Higher Consciousness, this is what is referred to as a harmonic convergence. Wherever consciousness aligns in rapport, this is a harmonic convergence. Group Soul effort aligned in single-pointed focus without any discord or disruption of the resonance of intent is another form of harmonic convergence.

Whereas the tools of the trade of construction on the fourth dimensional plane are that of hammers and nails, lumber and pipe, brick and mortar, the tools of creation become more refined as resonance is lifted to the fifth, sixth and seventh dimensional frequencies.

The Cities of Light will be constructed through the use of harmonics. Harmonics are used during the one-pointed focus of the Group Soul to manifest the Light into form through the use of sound/color. Prior to this phase of harmonic creation, the Group Soul effort will construct prototypes of communities through the initial practices of harmonics. Initially it is about setting the tone. What we mean by this is to hold the resonance at the heights of spiritual integrity, and this sets the tone for the outcome of manifestation. Creation can only bring forth that of its likeness. War torn landscapes are created from the source of anger, hatred, hurt and acts of divisiveness. How can it not be then that the Cities of Light must be created through the valuing of human dignity in accord with peace through harmony? A peaceful Soul walks a peaceful landscape. The communities will evolve through experimentation of the Group Soul efforts.

Nothing in creation is permanent or guaranteed in its outcome, as all things are made manifest on the shifting tides of energy and consciousness, nor are the Temples of the Soul erected to be permanent. Even the word foundation can be considered a misnomer that may mislead if the ego is allowed to interpret. Perhaps a Temple of the Soul will be built with the pure energy of whoever comes together in sacred ceremonial circle and will dissipate as soon as the circle disperses. Perhaps individuals will stand at the four corners and pillars emanating the energies of resonance to bring about the manifestation of the temple through "enactment" only of the energies. Further yet perhaps individuals from around the global community will focus their consciousness to create a global Temple of the Soul emanating the energies of the spiritual essences. Do you now see how you limit yourself to the fourth dimension thinking that you need wood and nails to create? Do not get caught in the ego's game of the fourth dimensional merry-go-round. You have arrived on a new ground of being, which is nothing like the one you have just left. Everything is new for you are renewed and are continuously being renewed.

The fundamentals of the qualitative spiritual essences mentioned herein are also subject to evolution. There is always more knowledge to acquire, more beauty to behold, more gratitude to beget even more gratitude and so forth. Grace is not a static state of being anymore than truth for all is ever paradoxically shifting and changing upon the backdrop of a sea of changelessness. Evolving implies motion or the movement of consciousness. It is not the same movement that you perceive within the fourth dimensional frequencies of revolution. Evolution occurs in the intangible essence first and foremost and then follows through in the manifestation of new form. All is an experiment through the creation and reflection upon the creation. We reiterate once again that the outcome of evolution is not entirely predetermined but is wholly dependent on conscious participation. Creation is the miracle that awaits the beholding by the creator within the creation. Be advised that until the individual Soul awakens to a certain degree of embodying the refined essences to become the walking Temple of the Soul, and henceforth awakens to the Group Soul harmony, this next phase of the plan will be delayed. It is all up to you. Figuratively, we place the scepter of power once more before you and urge you to take it in hand. We cannot hold the scepter of your own power. We can only hold our scepter of power figuratively higher to teach through our own example. We ever and a day offer to stand beside you and co-create, but we cannot wave our scepter of power and perform the miracles that many of you demand of us for that would rob you of your own power. Never would we usurp your power but merely guide you to claim it of yourself. When you come to more fully understand your power, you will learn to apply it to the task of harmonic creation.

Harmonic creation consists of varying levels of sound/ color, which we will refer to as tonal radiant emanations. A harmonic is a pattern of frequencies based on the coordinates of intersecting points of Light. We will explain how this works, although it is somewhat premature in preparation of these principles to be applied to your plane to coagulate matter in crystallized form. However, by offering you a glimpse into these creation principles, we wish to stir your consciousness to take the initial steps to arrive at this preparation point to utilize the harmonics of creation. It is also to be noted that the application of these principles of harmonics has already accomplished great success on the etheric levels by the workers in the Light through group meditation techniques. Utilizing these principles of harmonics in Group Soul meditative effort initially raises the resonance of the individual consciousness, as well as the Group Soul. These spiritual practices are merely the beginning of group work unification of efforts towards group creation.

When the point is approached of true harmony and one-pointed focus within the Group Effort, this energy can be directed to crystallize form in the external manifestation process. The Group Soul awakens to the level of harmonics pertinent to the energy essence to be manifested in form. Each individual within the group holds their resonant tone and together the harmonious tones bring forth the manifestation of idealistic vision in an accelerated manner. As a group, their consciousness is directed in the one-pointed focus aligned with the pattern of frequencies that are coordinated with the Master Creator's grid template. If there is but one in the Group who wavers on the edge of fear or self-doubt, the harmonic balance can be greatly disrupted and the form of the creation will either be distorted or aborted.

When we speak of holding the tone, we do not necessarily imply that there will always be the externalization of sound frequencies. Although that is one way to manipulate and coagulate matter, it is but the very beginnings of understanding the laws of resonant frequency. Group vocal toning is a preliminary exercise to bring about group harmony and raising resonant frequency. Harmonic tones coalesce matter while discordant tones disperse matter. Even within the discordant frequencies of your dimensional plane, Divine Love at the Heart of matter holds itself in form all the while as the law of entropy creates the friction of disintegration. That is how powerful your creation abilities are. Do you not see that you are still able to hold the things in your world in manifestation even through the discordant energies of fear tearing at its fabric continuously? That is the power of Source energy that you are currently utilizing even unconsciously. Now imagine harnessing this energy at Source consciously through Group Soul effort to bring forth the images of Divine Love made manifest in all its glorious beauty. Holding the resonance of consciousness at the vibrations of the template of the Soul essences described herein creates the necessary tonal radiant emanations to create the new form at ever increasing levels of frequency vibration. Even within the beginning stages of holding these higher resonating frequencies of the traits of the Temple of the Soul aforementioned in this volume the external manifestation will begin to shift accordingly. The immediate external environment will be a clear reflection of these traits once enough of the Group Soul embodies them. Members within the Group Soul will reflect to each other the higher essences. Welcome will be the homecoming of long strides accomplished as the Group Soul unites in their efforts. Through the very combination of Group Soul energies, the harmony of their effort flows with greater ease and greater accomplishment. Infusing the

Light that is Divine Love through telepathic rapport into the elements of creation on the fourth dimensional through the seventh dimensional frequencies will bring about another accelerated phase of awakening. This will be witnessed in bursts of creativity, a greater understanding of the higher sciences and sacred geometry, a greater knowledge of the properties of Light that is sound vibration and forces beyond your current understanding of nature that we can only allude to.

Beyond these initial understandings and application of the harmonics of the Temple of the Soul qualities, will come the greater understanding of how to directly harness the higher frequencies in the focus of one-pointed consciousness to move matter to degrees far beyond your current comprehension. Primarily the understanding of the principles of the higher sciences will only be bestowed upon those that are prepared to approach the energies of creation without being annihilated from the sheer power of these forces. Secondarily, no one will be allowed to approach an understanding of these forces without being in the highest mindset of not misusing them. Your planet is under the auspices of protection from the Ascended Host against any such violations. When any individual or Group Soul effort has attained the inherent integrity of self-governance abiding in the one Cosmic law "with harm to none," then and only then does the individual and Group Soul graduate to the understandings of these higher forces at play. Therefore, the precise instructions on how to create a City of Light through the use of Group Soul harmonics will not be offered in any handbook or manual. This knowledge can and only will be imparted by the Ascended Host and accessed within through the pathways of internal initiations of mastery. Even in the times of the three destruction phases of the isle called Atlantis, those misusing this power did not destroy the greater portions of earth, but a mere continent in the midst of an ocean that in its immensity swallowed it back into the depths of the unconscious. You may now see how the protective shield of Divine Love is ever sheathed around the glorious being sometimes called Gaia through the auspices of the Ascended Host and the planetary logos, Sanat Kumara.

It is of great import for the workers in the Light to understand that this process of crystallized form manifestation is done through the seventh dimensional creation process. We offer this to you as a guideline to see how much of your individual and Group Soul conscious focus this takes to bring forth. Ever is the process ongoing before the Group Soul will step forth into the creation of the crystallized Cities of Light. Do not be discouraged for the greatest endurance of patience will always bring forth the greatest rewards.

Crystalline essences in the lattice grid work are activated on the meridian points of the layers of bodies. Crystal clear is not just a catch phrase in your world, but holds the clues of a higher truth. Crystal energy amplifies all avenues of flowing energies. When the avenues of energy are clear, the crystal energy will amplify more clarity. Cities built upon the crystalline structure of the lattice grid work will amplify the living libraries of the Language of Light to other dimensional realms. Understanding of the crystalline structure is to comprehend the nature of fusion and merging into a unified whole of the living conscious being that is always becoming more. Refinement is key in this work to create the crystalline essence within the four-body system to align with the crystalline essence of the earth body and the star essence of the twelve-body system. Each alignment of the energetic frequencies brings greater alignment within the multidimensional spheres of creation. What we mean by this is that at each stage of alignment, it opens up the portals to more dimensional frequencies, which then again must be harmonically attuned and so forth.

Harmonic resonance reflects its likeness. Group Soul resonating at the vibration of wisdom will bring more wisdom into effect in the world. This will impress the collective consciousness to transmute ignorance into higher knowledge. Likewise, Group Soul resonating at the vibration of integrity will bring the value of human dignity to the Light of conscious attention. Group Soul resonating at the vibration of faith will bring more trust in the world. Group Soul resonating at the vibration of tranquility will bathe the world in a sea of serenity. Within the Law of Elegance, no one will be required to move boulders with a hand tool, for that goes against the very nature of the Almighty Divine Source of the pure powers of creation. Lifted high upon the vibration of Love will be the structure of the new creation. How could the Almighty Divine Source not pour forth and share its omnipotence? Almighty Divine Source of creation does not struggle to radiate its glory, power or magnitude. It simply is glorious, powerful and magnificent, and thus so are you for you are made of the same energetic essence. Who of you will step forth and shine in the glory of your powerful magnificence?

Imagine if you will the Group Soul holding the idealized vision with all clarity and complete diligence to the focus. Imagine if you will the Group Soul harnessing the powerful energies of Source to direct this idealized vision into manifestation through one-pointed consciousness through the points of the Group merkaba. Then imagine if you will the idealized vision manifesting without so much as a hammer or tool being lifted. Imagine if you will that as long as the Group Soul along with the Ascended Host holds the vision it remains intact, but as the idealized vision expands or outgrows its purpose the manifestation too will shift. It is precisely how things are manifested in your current dimensional experience, except for the fact that the ideas that are made manifest are not precisely aligned with idealized vision. In addition, the law of entropy is not something that humanity has awakened to overcome. Ideas at the fourth dimensional level are meant to break down to make way for the idealized vision to take its place. Fear creates fearful images. Self-denial creates lack for to deny the self is to deny the powers of creation. Rather than gently shifting the external manifestation through evolvement of the ideal, it is fear and erosion of the ideas on your plane that allows your world to be destroyed and crumble into ages past. A gentle shift towards the ideal far outshines the atrocities of human suffering created through fear. Idealized vision is illuminated by the Light within rather than reflected on the limitations of dimensional surfaces. As the Group Soul holds an idealized vision in the harmonic resonance of vibration, the vision is crystallized through the refined Light frequency. It begins with work in the etheric realm first and foremost to understand the principles of resonance and the power of Group Soul effort to shift the resonance to higher frequencies. Idealized vision is the ultimate truth of the spiritual essence and all focus must be toward attaining the ideal. Ideals are born from the Light but into the shadows they fall. Let it be known and fully understood that the manifestation of ideas within the limitations of the fourth dimensional creation fields will always fall far short of the ideal. Raising the resonance to the higher dimensional vibrations is the process to refine the ideas into the ideal. At each level of increased frequency of vibration the shadows begin to disappear in the Light. Manifested form in the fourth dimensional frequencies is reflected light. Ideals can be recognized by their inherent luminosity. The more Light something exudes the closer to the ideal is the creation. Enlightenment is a term that means much more than the average aspirant can initially comprehend. Once again we urge you to learn to walk before you run. Learning is to understand the process otherwise you will not be able to repeat the process.

We will speak to you regarding self-governance. This is an area that awaits the proper timing of event sequencing for the greatest alignment to the highest integrity is needed to elicit this type of environment on a planetary scale. The human that behaves as the animal in its viciousness must adhere to the limitations of enforced rules and regulations until such time as the human awakens to the evolved state of the spiritual human being. The dense patterns of human nature that reflect lust, greed, survival tactics, territorial motives, control and manipulation all need to be transmuted through refinement. Manmade laws are made for unruly men to abide by as a learning process, but the evolved spiritual human being is self-governed and answers to the Cosmic law, which is harmlessness in all word and deed. Awakened souls reach an evolutionary stage where actions and behavior are attuned to the highest spiritual essences. When a person resonates with integrity, there is no need to design laws to abide by for spiritual integrity is its own form of self-governance. There will be no abuse of power to bend or manipulate man made laws when everyone arrives at this stage of evolvement. When a person resonates with truth, there is no need to create falsehoods to hide their errors in judgment behind. As each person awakens to resonate with empathy, all taking of life for any purposes will cease and desist. Each life will be self-governed and empowered to choose transition to other dimensions of their own act of free will without karmic interference for the karma of cause and effect will return rather quickly to reveal its imbalances. With each individual awakening to the intuitive faculties, miscommunication and misinterpretations will be avoided. For the person of integrity, there will be no stepping over of boundaries and full respect is given to each and another. Placing trust in the Higher Self leaves no space for the experience of betrayal or deceit. As wisdom is employed the arrogance of self-righteousness will be eliminated. With more knowledge acquired, the humble knower will know that he/she will never know it all. With each person walking in the grace and dignity of their natural state of being, clumsiness in all areas of life will be a way of the past. No one will step on another's toes either figuratively or literally, which also goes to say that there will be no more collisions or accidents. Sensing the energy of each other and moving in harmonious rapport allows no room for haphazard events to manifest. As each person awakens to wonder and amazement, joy will spontaneously shimmer. Each act of kindness will increase the level of compassion and dissolve the distinction of separation. When the community awakens in Group Soul effort as equals in all rights, there will be no class distinctions to keep any human being repressed. Creation will be a rhythmic flow of energy that is both powerfully consciously manifested as well as synchronistically spontaneous.

We will speak to you of the ease of elegance and grace. Under the state of grace everything flows with ease. Directing the will through the state of grace is effortless for all of your highest dreams are granted fulfillment. The Law of Elegance assures that the maximum is accomplished through the minimum of energy expended. We suggest you hasten your alignment with this ease and elegance that is your true nature. Everyone has come into being through the state of grace which means that no penalty is inflicted for any of your perceived errors of judgment, and each and everyone will return consciously to the center of Source by the same means. Struggle is merely a by-product of the ego's resistance. Forgiveness is a component of the state of grace. Self-forgiveness and forgiveness of others is the key to unlock the door to grace. It is only the ego once again that resists forgiving and being forgiven. Nothing is difficult other than that which you portend it to be. Discipline is not the same as struggle. Ever and always must you be diligent in your single-pointed focus to disallow the ego's voice to override that of your own higher knowing. You are the prophets of your own destiny within each powerful moment. Does your voice hearken the prophecy of doom and gloom or does it bode well of the glorious angelic message of heaven made manifest?

Within the mineral, plant and animal kingdom, you will witness also an elevated evolution of consciousness. This is not to say that the animals of the land or the fowl of the air will acquire human traits, but rather that they will reflect clearly the higher essence of the spiritual human being. When the spiritual human being evolves beyond the animal nature, any viciousness enacted through the animal level will cease and desist. The lion will lie down with the lamb, for the spiritual human being will have ceased warring with it's own nature and that of all nature. All species of the other kingdoms will reflect this peaceful nature. Fear and aggression of the human animal nature is what is reflected in these kingdoms presently. When the human kingdom stops attacking each other, there will be no fear from the attacks of wild animals. When the poison bite of words from the human tongue is tempered, there will be no fear of a poison sting from an insect or reptile. The only war of the human being with nature is the war waged upon its own nature. Only after humanity arrives at the complete surrender of the ego to the Higher Self will fear fade from your world, and only then will heaven be created on earth. This is the ascension of which your prophets have heralded. Raising the resonance of the emotions and thoughts beyond the fearful images into the realms of higher frequencies of the qualities of the Soul is the only road to this accomplishment. Fear does not exist in the Heart and upon the breath of the Higher Self. No word uttered forth from the voice of the Higher Self ever gives breath to the illusion of fear. If you hear the voice of fear, know that it is the voice of the limiting ego. Banish this voice that speaks of fear for this is the ploy of the ego's temptations.

That which we refer to as Gaia consciousness of the earth sphere also has a higher aspect of consciousness in the one called Sanat Kumara. Among the myriad of focal points of Sanat Kumara is the focus of ever expanding and ascending the consciousness of Gaia through harmonic convergence. Humanity must also attune its consciousness in the harmonic convergence with Gaia.

What is a model of harmonic living? A model is a representation. What will each of you represent? Who among you will sing forth the sound of harmony amidst the sea of droning chaos? Who among you will walk in the state of grace? Who among you will walk boldly through the shadows of fear? Who among you will hold their resonance ever reaching to the heights of the purity of Divine Love?

Would thou go forth into the world and suffer the little children? Would thou go forth into the world with an angry fist raised? Would thou go forth into the world with an armored vessel of domination? Would thou go forth into the world with anger in your words? All conflict whether a domestic quarrel or world war shatters harmony. All conflict begins within the hearts and mind of humanity and extends into the world. If you want peace, you must hold the peace within. We avow that thou would serve best to seek the peace in the kingdom within and hence go forth into the world to bring the peace of eternity to reign upon the land. Until the first one begins to make haste to these ends, will others wait to follow?

Be present in your world and represent the essence of your Soul. Be the model of harmonic living and others will bear witness to the truth in your actions and find comfort in the wisdom of your words.

SEVEN

THY KINGDOM COME

*There is no time like the present to be
fully in the presence of the new creation.*

There is no poverty but that which withholds the giving and receiving of Love. Nothing is lost when the kingdom is gained. To be the kingdom is to enact the kingdom. To enact the kingdom is to participate fully conscious in the new creation.

The World Server is asked to sacrifice the needs of the ego, but it is no real sacrifice to trade in the Soul's suffering for joy. Likewise, there is no real sacrifice to trade in the devastation and tragedy of war for the peace that is brought about through harmony. Where is the great loss to trade in self-imposed limitations for more freedom of spiritual expression? Will you continue down the dead-end and well-trodden path of the ego rather than soar on the wings of the dove? Will you plod through the density of your own fear-based creations or ascend to heaven's glory?

Providence is the road that leads you home. Shelter in the arms of the Divine is your protection ever and always. Fear is only a shadow that the ego casts upon your path. Why must ye of the Light continue to cower from the illusions of your own paltry shadow? Images of fear are but wisps of smoke that disappear in a brightly sun filled sky. Visions of beauty shine in the Light of the eternal. Would you choose to serve images of fear over that of the visions of beauty? Bring forth the visions of beauty upon the landscape and see the reflection of your own true countenance.

To prepare the way is to be the way. A welcome home is only a reminder that you never left. That which is sought is gained tenfold, but that which is waylaid is but the ego's decoy. There is no war other than war with your self. Hence go forth to meet your self and make peace right away.

Prayer asks for that which you feel you cannot accomplish or attain. Claiming your power is the answer and fulfillment to all of your prayers. Prayer is only the prelude to knowing it is already accomplished. Prayer sets the tone for humility in receiving, but knowing it is already accomplished brings about the desired results. It is not to say that prayer should be negated or neglected but to understand that it is just one step along your path to learn of the humility that brings you to the center point of the full mastery of knowing. Humility is powerful for it is through humility that you recognize the true power at Source. Like children playing with fire, it is always best to approach the power at Source with great humbleness as you learn to harness the potent powers of creation with harm to none. When a greater understanding of power is realized, even the Master bows in awe before the presence of its Source for it is within that very understanding that power reveals itself to be infinitely omnipotent. So we say to you, those who are able to approach the Inner Sanctum will only do so in great humility for to do otherwise will keep the gates to the outer courtyards bolted and locked through your own ego arrogance. It is an assault in the face of Divine Love for any ego's arrogance to claim omnipotence, for to claim such is to show forth the ignorance of the ego's limitations. Therefore, the ego must be humbled while the Higher Self exudes the power of creation through the Love that is Divine. To sit at the threshold of the Holy of Holies is to accept your scepter of power upon the thrones of the principalities. Those who sit in powerful command on the thrones of the principalities hold governance over the many creation fields. Do not wait to be invited, for you will linger in trepidation at heaven's gate. Whosoever stands bold in the Light inherits the kingdom, and whosoever inherits the kingdom acquires the power to bring forth its rewards. Those who give the rewards away in the humble sharing that is the truth of mastery are the wealthiest of the wealthy. Intangible gifts are far more precious in their essence than all the belongings the ego bargains for. Be alert that the ego is the reflective part of you that is always longing for more belongings and is unaware that it is really only longing to belong to the wholeness that is Divine Love at Source. Welcome your Self home in the arms of your own Divinity.

Popularity is the notoriety of the personal ego, but glory is the hallmark of the saint. A saint can walk among thieves and not be robbed. Likewise, thieves can sit among saints and be repentant. Penance is the revolving door of self-punishment, while sincere forgiveness is the elevator. Misery loves company but whose company does it keep? It is deemed better to be in the company of one visionary dreamer than a million cynics. A visionary dreamer has the gift of inspiration to impart, but a cynic will rob you blind of your own inner sight and leave you bereft. Being in the presence of a saint is a rare gift to be treasured for saints are a rare treasure in your world. Who among you have made your mark on the world as a saint? Each stride towards saintliness is a step well taken. Strength of purpose is strength of mind, body and Soul. When these three are aligned, accomplishment of truth is at hand.

A Heart on fire is far more warming than the rays of a million suns. Purity of Heart and mind is purity of the Soul. If once a Heart be broken in two, it will Love twice as strong. Love is flexible and flows like water over rock. It is the ego that resists being bathed in Love's soothing waters. When the dam of the ego's making breaks free, the pure waters will flow forth once more across the arid landscape of consciousness. Now do you see which part of your little mind invented and inflicts damnation? Words hold more powerful resonance and meaning than you can still grasp with your minds. Do you not yet see how "The Word" itself will bind you or will free you? Whichever meaningful words you give your will over to will either bind you or set you free. All words have meaning encoded in their numeric formulas. All is number. All is resonant frequency. Resonate to the frequency of Divine Love, and Divine Love is its own reward. Speak forth only words that uplift and regenerate. Speak forth only words that resonate the truth, and the truth shall set you free.

Weariness is but a nuisance of the negative mind. How can there be truth in weariness when the energy of creation is infinite and self-sustaining? Step into the fountain of unceasing energy at Source to rejuvenate your Spirit and nourish your Soul. Then try and deny the power that courses through your multidimensional bodies. Replenishment is ever a gift you can indulge in, as refreshment is its complement.

Those who waver upon the battle lines of indecision are fearful of their power to choose so the choice is made for them by the limiting voice of the ego. Confinement to this cage does not keep you safe but only keeps you from your own freedom.

Invite only happiness in where sadness lurks at your

door. Leave the door wide open when Love comes knocking, but let not sorrow take one step over the threshold. Wallow not in the shallow waters of self-pity but sink to the depths of eternal Love to land upon the shores of evermore. Where you are going sorrow cannot enter. Where you have been sadness knows the way. Which footsteps will you walk in and which are truly your own?

Wishing is fanciful but knowing is supreme. Wish not, waste not, for wishing is a waste of energy. Wonder never ceases when amazement is its companion. Cravings cannot be satiated but passion is its own fulfillment. All illusions of paucity are shattered through gaining the kingdom.

Who of you can say you are truly ever alone? One is never alone when the One is embodied everywhere. In the eyes of the other is the reflection of the self. In the Eye of God is the truth that you are. This Eye that is all seeing is all knowing. This Eye is your eye for there is only One. When you arrive at the center of this truth you will know that there is always more to know. Paradox abounds and this is the wonder of knowing you will always arrive right back where you begin and to begin again is to have never left. This is the beautiful dance that is the power of creation.

Pettiness is best ignored for to give it attention is what the ego desires. To serve the ego's desire is the disempowerment of your powerful truth at Source. The only illusion is the ego's limited perceptions. All else is real. Remove the veil of illusion that your ego covers upon your eyes that see double and behold the reality of the singular power that awaits your command.

Mistakes are only the bane of ill begotten thoughts run amok. Would thou entertain thoughts of darkness when Love ever beckons you to the safety of its Light? Every word counts, and every action has its consequence. Will you be The Word in manifestation that speaks the truth or cower in the shadows of deceiving yourself from the truth of your very own essential nature? Who of all of you will command The Word to be sent forth to do your bid on behalf of the Ascended Host and the Almighty Source of Creation? Where are the courageous ones that dare to step out of the shadows of their own unconscious makings? When the Legions of Light are assembled will your name be among them?

The signs and symbols are impressed upon your brow. Symbols will lead you home. Like familiar landmarks along the way let them reveal your truth. A million lies will never add up to one truth. Don't give credence where credence is not merited. Give due honor where honor is due. Likewise, receive due honor where honor is due. What you give to others you give to your Self, but know this to not just be another catch phrase of the ages for this is the truth in all actions set forth. Your thoughts and emotions are like boomerangs, and why is it that when they come back to hit you on the head, you blame someone else for tossing them? Send out Love and when it comes to caress your weary head and rest it on the shoulders of strength, will you then see that it is your own spiritual fortitude that you stand upon and find refuge in? You are made of the very substance of Divine Love, and when you look to the Masters you will see that we already celebrate your existence in harmony. We patiently await each moment you come closer to this truth. We ever walk alongside you even though you relegate us to the shadows of mystery. We proclaim that it is you that are the mystery, for you are the new creation that has never been and the heavens await your arrival.

Externalization of the kingdom assures that no one goes

for want. Walk in the land of plenty, and there is nothing for want. As each being quells their anger, where will there be room for enemies? As each individual stands in the center of their own empowerment, who will be left to abuse their personal power and hold their power sway over others? As each being steps out of the shadows of fear and into the brilliance of the Light, where will fear find a home?

The rewards of the World Server are greater beyond your most fanciful imaginings. Gifts of the Soul cannot be measured in numbers for the Soul is the landscape of infinity. Rewards of the Heart far outshine the temporary temptations of ego desire. Temptation is the poison of the temporal world. Rectitude is the antidote. The greatest rewards come from the least amount of effort, for the Great Work is fueled by Cosmic energy. This does not mean that the tasks will be few and far between. The Great Work is ever upon you both in leisure and in task but this does not imply struggle. Energy employed towards the goal of Divine Plan is aligned with the Source. Reaping a bounty must not be the focal point when the aim is towards uplifting. Bounty and plenitude are the inherent nature of the Source. The worker in the Light aligned with the Source already has everything they need to carry out the work. Rise to the occasion and collect your rewards. A high resonance reflects a bountiful existence. We do not imply this to mean that you need more wealth than you can distribute, for unless you can distribute all wealth fairly and evenly, why would you need to acquire more than you need? You cannot receive but that which is no more than that which you can contain and once more give forth. This is the Law of Creation. As all is energy, you can only manifest to the degree of power that your consciousness can contain and harness the energy. To be the planetary body you must be able to

147

contain all of the energy inherent within the creation of a planet within your conscious focus. By this we do not refer to simply the limitations of the four dimensions and the four kingdoms of the earth plane. There are far more energies at play than you can witness through the eyes that see double. The limitations of your own boundaries are the limits of your supply. We speak of the rewards of the Soul and of the means to create more beauty in the world not necessarily more meaningless things. A thing of beauty is a thing to behold, but anything less is wasted space where true beauty could takes its place. With grace you shall proceed to walk through the garden, and the garden will blossom underneath your feet. Joy will spring from the fountains, where once the sorrow did flow.

Ingenuity is the mother of the new creation. Proficiency is the father. Beauty is the offspring. In the depths of beauty are treasures rare and unique to each individuated Soul. Merging these treasures together in Group Soul effort sires an entire garden of blossoming hues. Idealized vision shines in the Light of the infinite and splashes across eternity in a prism array of crystallized form. Crystalline bodies within the crystal Cities of Light refract and reflect the brilliance of the beautiful colors of creation made manifest. Truth that shines clarity shines in the eye that is singular. Merging and mingling of spiritual essences re-emerge as the new creation. Glory be to all made manifest in the Light that is Divine Love.

In your world, many view money as the value that is placed upon anything that is deemed of use or of service. There is nothing inherently wrong with valuing the energy of exchange through goods or services. Understand that it is but a reflection and lesson to learn the value of worth. Values reflect their worth. What is the value of beauty, grace, dignity or integrity?

What is the worth of intuition, knowledge, truth or wisdom? We are here to tell you that they are worth their weight in silver and gold, but we do not refer to the precious metals mined from the bosom of your earth. Why do you suppose the gold and silver hold a high price in your world? What gives them the value that humanity seeks? Can you not see the clarity of the solar Gold Light and the lunar Silver Light that blends in the sacred alchemy to create the very essence of your being? Stop and ponder just when it was that the ego has transferred the value of the spiritual essence inherent in the human being onto the metals mined from the earth? Why do you suppose a diamond is placed in high value? Having transformed and transmuted from coal to precious gem, it reflects clearly the many facets of the One. The emergence of the diamond from the coal teaches the creation miracle of transformation, transmutation and transfiguration. Clarity of truth is a beauty beyond any limitations of value. What is the precious value of the human life? How is it that human life has come to be so devalued? When brother rises against brother and claims the land as bounty, who among you will claim the kingdom within? Shift your perception of values and worth, and the kingdom will be made manifest. Rise above the status quo to set a new standard of values and worth. Be the valuable and worthy one and treat everyone likewise. Precious are those that see the spiritual value in all things. Blessed are those that see the beauty of the Soul reflected in all things. Wondrously wealthy are those that feel the bounty of Love flowing forth from the Heart of Hearts. Pure are those that walk in the clear Light of unconditional Love.

Within the task accomplished are the rewards you seek. The worker in the wilderness will find sustenance in the sweet breath of garden nectars. The worker who labors long in the garden will find rest as their reward. Whosoever digs deep to plant seeds will uncover the treasures of the Soul. The worker who weeds out negative thoughts will find the clarity of ultimate truth. Whosoever prunes the tree reaps the most fruit in its season. Those who walk gently upon the land will make the most impact. The worker with the diligence to see all things through will see clearly through all things. Those that push forcefully to move the obstinate boulders will discover the ease of surrender and release. Whichever worker reaches the finish line first will be the first to move the finish lines of imaginary boundaries even further. Since there is no finish line, expansion of consciousness is its own reward forever and each day. Those who stretch the muscles of consciousness will gain the strength of their spiritual fortitude. Those who are reverent are the revered. Whosoever walks in the brilliance of their Light will cast no shadow. Those who speak the highest truth will see through all lies. The one who seeks is the one that is found. Whosoever shall claim their full creative power will inherit the throne at the threshold of the Holy of Holies to take their rightful place as a Master Creator God being.

The fruits of your labor are to be shared with all for there is no lack or want in the kingdom made manifest. There is nothing that another has that you need for all that you need springs forth from the Source within to pour upon the land. In the external manifestation of the kingdom, all that is required is to offer and receive the many gifts of Love. Being attuned to the One Source is to be resourceful. Resources are abundant and eternal. Nothing is lacking in the kingdom other than your own faith and trust in the Source of all creation. How is it that a tree sprouts from the seed and brings forth an endless supply of fruit? The fruit once more drops its seeds in the soil to bring forth a new life. Within the seed of the fruit of life is the reality of the endless abundance that creation is. The man who owns one fruit tree is as rich as the man who owns an orchard for all one man needs is one fruit tree to continue the life cycles of creation. How is it that the wind blows through the tree rustling the leaves? How is it that you are conscious and alive? Life is the gift that keeps giving more life. Life springs forth from life. Eternal life springs forth from Divine Source and Divine Source is alive and well. Your life and consciousness springs forth from Divine Source so, therefore, you are alive and well. How long will you continue to deny your eternal and infinite Divinity? How long will you continue to deny the abundance that life is? When you embody this as truth you will be the one to fulfill the prophecies. We do not mean to imply that you need to seek the money and riches of your world. Material riches are a reflection that the Source is ever abundant and giving. It is our way of showing you that you already lay claim to the kingdom of abundance that life is for you are life itself. You are the solution to all your endeavors for you are the solar fire. You are the essence for you are the response to your Soul's deepest desire.

When the Master steps forth the waves shall part. We make reference of the resonant waves of harmonic frequency, as well as the metaphoric analogy with the miracles of the Masters that came before you. A Master conducts the waves to create a symphony, as well as parting the sea of consciousness to make new paths home. What you may perceive as abstract concept, the Master sees as reality. Shift your perception and see through the eye that is singular, and the waves of harmonic resonance will sing a new song. New words with a new resonance will echo the refrain and build upon the waves to manifest in the creation fields of the new dawn and the new day. Make your song a lull-a-bye of intention to soothe the angry and hurting. Lift your voice upon the resonant waves and sing the world into harmony. Make a way station for the Soul to find its rest and reprieve from your long suffering. Be the color palette of the new creation and splash yourself across the void in ever changing hues.

What once was is no more in the history of repetition for the cycles have been transcended. What will be is the will to be infinitely and eternally. This is the key to your mastery, and you hold the key.

Wherever you see need, fulfill it. Wherever you see the hungry, offer sustenance. Wherever you see the wounded, heal their wounds. Wherever you see heartache, soothe it. Wherever you see tears, dry them. Wherever you see fears, ease them. Wherever you see loneliness, offer friendship. Wherever you see suffering, ease the pain. Wherever you see the downtrodden, uplift their spirits. Wherever you see wantonness, hold your vision higher. Wherever you see thoughtlessness, be thoughtful. Wherever you see ignorance, offer wisdom. Wherever you see corruption, be just. Wherever you see emptiness, fill it with meaning. Wherever you see loss, bring forth abundance. Wherever you see lies, be the truth. Wherever you see ugliness, create beauty.

There is a solution to every need. There is a fulfillment to every longing. You are the solution. You are the fulfillment. You are the gift. You are the reward. You are the power to transform your world. You have everything you need at your fingertips. Within the Heart of Hearts is a treasure trove of gifts to bring forth into the world. Step forward oh ye who are to birth the new formation for you are *in-formation*. You are the living libraries of the wisdom of the ages that were already and the wisdom yet to be born.

The treasures are already available to you, but you must claim them. They must be claimed from within and brought forth to your world, thus ensuring the externalization of the kingdom. Paths in the kingdom are paved with the Golden bricks of solar illumination, and the multidimensional fabric is braided with the Silver cords of truth. Yours is the kingdom for now and evermore. The scepter of power is now in your hand. Will you raise it high above your head or hide it in your cloak of earthly delights? Masters are not created in a day, yet it takes only a moment to attain mastery. Power is in the moment of choice. Each moment of choice births worlds within worlds. Each world is a multidimensional universe. Truth is in the paradox just as paradox gives birth to truth.

Happiness is the prelude to joy. Joy gives birth to ecstatic bliss, which ripples in the pools of eternity pulsing out the harmonic rhythm of creation. Each layer of conscious evolution builds on these foundations and exponentially increases in intensity. Light builds upon Light and refracts and reflects brighter still. Light makes up the building blocks of creation, and it is to this truth that you will come to know and embody. What will you build upon the new foundation of being?

Prosperity is the Cosmic design for what is there in all of creation that cannot flourish in a Love so Divine? Your roots are watered in the depths of your Soul, now will your Spirits bring forth the fruits from this tree of life? From the deep still waters pour forth an endless tide of blessings.

Beatitude becomes you. Diamonds of clarity shine in your mind's eye. Wellsprings of wisdom wash over your feet as you walk the path of knowing. Purity of heart cleanses the waters of life, and the waters of life flow forth to nurture the land.

Joy resounds with its echoing refrain forever and a day. Peace through harmony is its song. Lift the voice of your Soul to sing, and witness the colorful tones of the new creation. You are the new creation. Walk now anew through the bountiful garden of idealized dreams made manifest.

Within the Golden solar Light of the Great Central Sun the Soul is bathed in its glorious raiment. Walk in the Golden raiment of the Light that you are and are always becoming. Shine your radiant splendor in its fullest glory. The Light that is and ever shall be forever shines its brilliance, and you will always and forever add Light to the Light that is already.

The Golden Cities are in the palm of your hand. The power of creation awaits your command. You are the Light that your world awaits. Be the truth, walk the truth, live the truth and the truth will be known. Step into mastery. Know.

It is already accomplished.

Message From
MASTER CREATOR GOD
THOTH

I AM Thoth of the Golden Solar Light and the Silver reflecting eye. I AM Hermes Trismegistus, the thrice born, Master of the trinity of creation, as I AM Master over the creation fields of multiple universes. As your fathers and mothers taught you to take the first steps to walk, so do I, as your Father of Light, teach you the steps to become the Master that walks in the Light. Walk with me through the Halls of Amenti, and I will shine for you the Light that you are becoming. Walk with me through the Halls of Amenti, and I will show you the power of the scepter to command the breath upon the waters. Look upon your brow through the eye that is singular and know the symbols of the Words of Power, for these are the words that cause your very breath to be cast upon your manifestation field. Know these things to be truth and you will begin to know the power of creation that is at your command. Walk with me now, and I will clothe you in the Light of your own awakening. Yours is the power to command the Light upon the darkness. Yours is the power to bring Divine Love to its fullest expression. Walk with me in the Light of the Divine One, and you shall walk in peace forevermore.

Message From
LORD SANANDA

    I AM Lord Sananda, the Christed One. Blessings be yours for you are the blessed ones. I AM the Light upon your way, as you are the beacon of my Heart. Wherever thou sincere Heart pours forth the longing, I AM the one who will always respond. I AM with you for now and always in your loneliness and your joys. I walk beside you in your suffering. Ask and I shall lift your weariness from you. Ask and I shall remove the burdens from your shoulders. Ask and I shall make your tasks Light. Ask and be willing always to receive through the Heart that is Divine. You are the blessed ones, yet you know not of your wealth and attributes. You are the humble ones, yet you know not of your powerful command. Walk not in the shade of fearful wanderings, but come to me in the Golden Light and you shall know that you are Divinely protected. I AM Lord Sananda, and I AM with you ever and a day in the Light of the Golden Ray.

Message From
SAINT GERMAIN

I AM Saint Germain of the Violet Flame, as I AM of many powerful names. Who of you do not exist by many names for such is not the limitation of the Divine Essence of your existence? Step into the Violet Flame and know who it is that speaks to you and of the transmutation energy of the Violet Flame, which shall consume all of your doubts and worries. Walk with me in harmony, and I shall show you how to walk in splendor. Oh magnificent One, who is it that beckons you to the doorstep of ill boding? It is not the message that the Masters hail, yet I AM here to tell you that it is of your own doing that suffering shall ensue. I AM here to tell you that it is of your own power that you shall cease all strife and suffering. Whenceforth the day shall come when you bid to end your ill begotten ways, I shall be with you also in the Light of your awakening.

> When once there was a garden,
> now does the garden grow?
> Who is it that does the planting
> of the fruits that you shall sow?

Message From
SANAT KUMARA
The Planetary Logos

I AM Sanat Kumara, Lord of the Earthly sphere and guardian of creation in these manifestation fields. The work you do is the work I AM concerned with for you are the heirs to the throne of this principality. I do not oft speak directly for I send my messengers to herald the shifting tides of conscious creation. You are each and every one held in my embrace, as you are each and every one held in the embrace of your forefathers, the Master Creator God beings. Hearken to this outcry, for it is of great import within the scheme of Divine Plan that you hasten to your tasks of awakening your conscious intent. With each choice you make, your impact is far more reaching than you can dare to imagine. With each thought you think, whether it is of the constricting and limiting vibration or of the expansive vibration, your impact is far more reaching than you can comprehend. With each emotion that you feel, whether it is of the angry or fearful kind or of the joy of ecstatic bliss, your impact is far more reaching than you can sense. I AM the Lord Sanat Kumara, and I beckon you hence to commit to the vigilance of watching over your every thought and deed. Step forth now and accept the inheritance of these principalities that are your Divine birthright. Sit beside me on the thrones of power and command the earth to hasten the ascension to attain the Light. Let it be so for so it is for now and evermore.

.

Glossary of Terms

The Law of Abundance – Consciousness can only contain and bring forth that of its like resonance. There is infinite energy at Divine Source but only the portion that each consciousness can embody of the Divine Source energy is that to which the creation will reflect its likeness.

The Law of Elegance – The minimum energy expended for the maximum return of its effect. The effect of one-pointed focus brings forth the maximum results from the minimum energy expended.

The Law of Resonance – Whenever two or more are gathered, the resonance of each person must be in agreement. If one person's energy is resonating at a higher rate, there are three possible outcomes: 1) The others in the room must raise their resonance to meet the person's higher vibration, or 2) the one person resonating at the higher rate must lower theirs to meet the lower vibration of the others, or 3) they must all adjust their resonance to meet somewhere in the middle. If anyone is unable to hold the higher resonance or lower their resonance to match those in the room, they will eventually remove themselves from the room due to discomfort or agitation.

ABOUT THE AUTHOR

Sharon Shane is a channeled intuitive, spiritual teacher and author.

Since 1997 she has written a series of online e-mail newsletters. Her poetry and articles have been published in numerous magazines.

Sharon has traveled to speak and teach workshops and offers online classes through the Internet. She has worked with a variety of indigenous healers and shaman from around the world to integrate their teachings and to promote the efforts of cross-cultural exchange.

In accord with the Ascended Masters, Sharon implemented the invitation for global participation of "The Great OM Event" in May of 2003 and was invited by the Mevlana Supreme Foundation to speak at "The Call to World Peace by the Universal Brotherhood" in Istanbul, Turkey, in November 2003. All spiritual work of Liquid Light Center aims to align with the Ascended Host in the unfolding of Divine Plan and to empower the individual towards mastery.

e-mail: info@sharonshane.com
web site: www.sharonshane.com

ABOUT THE COVER ARTIST

Juergen Neckenich, Artist and Designer, worked until 1997 as a freelancer for different German/French TV Broadcasts, and currently at his own company "n+t vision on screen." He created On-Air designs, many leaders, studio designs, graphics and web sites. His nonprofit company is "artura."

Juergen is creating mandalas and video animations for color/ sound healing, artwork, video and web sites for nonprofit organizations and companies, including the Liquid Light Center of Sharon Shane and LIGHTWORKER of Steve Rother.

www.arturanet.com/artura

Other books by Sharon Shane:

In the Garden of the Goddess
ISBN 0-9676968-0-1

Available through Liquid Light Center Publishing:

www.sharonshane.com